Blade Runner

Ridley Scott's *Blade Runner* is widely regarded as a 'masterpiece of modern cinema' and is regularly ranked as one of the great films of all time. Set in a dystopian future where the line between human beings and 'replicants' is blurred, the film raises a host of philosophical questions about what it is to be human, the possibility of moral agency and freedom in 'created' life forms, and the capacity of cinema to make a genuine contribution to our engagement with these kinds of questions.

This volume of specially commissioned chapters systematically explores and addresses these issues from a philosophical point of view. Beginning with a helpful introduction, the seven chapters examine the following questions:

- How is the theme of death explored in *Blade Runner* and with what implications for our understanding of the human condition?
- What can we learn about the relationship between emotion and reason from the depiction of the 'replicants' in *Blade Runner*?
- How are memory, empathy, and moral agency related in *Blade Runner*?
- How does the style and 'mood' of *Blade Runner* bear upon its thematic and philosophical significance?
- Is *Blade Runner* a meditation on the nature of film itself?

Including a brief biography of the director and a detailed list of references to other writings on the film, *Blade Runner* is essential reading for students – indeed anyone – interested in philosophy and film studies.

Contributors: Colin Allen, Peter Atterton, Amy Coplan, David Davies, Berys Gaut, Stephen Mulhall, C. D. C. Reeve.

Amy Coplan is Associate Professor and Chair of Philosophy at California State University, Fullerton, USA. She is the co-editor, with Peter Goldie, of *Empathy: Philosophical and Psychological Perspectives* (2011).

David Davies is Professor and Chair of Philosophy at McGill University, Canada. He is the author of *Art as Performance* (2004), *Aesthetics and Literature* (2007), and *Philosophy of the Performing Arts* (2011), and editor of *The Thin Red Line* (Routledge, 2008).

Philosophers on Film

In recent years, the use of film in teaching and doing philosophy has moved to centre stage. Film is increasingly used to introduce key topics and problems in philosophy, from ethics and aesthetics to epistemology, metaphysics and philosophy of mind. It is also acknowledged that some films raise important philosophical questions of their own. Yet until now, dependable resources for teachers and students of philosophy using film have remained very limited. *Philosophers on Film* answers this growing need and is the first series of its kind.

Each volume assembles a team of international contributors to explore a single film in depth, making the series ideal for classroom use. Beginning with an introduction by the editor, each specially commissioned chapter will discuss a key aspect of the film in question. Additional features include a biography of the director and suggestions for further reading.

Philosophers on Film is an ideal series for students studying philosophy and film, aesthetics, and ethics and anyone interested in the philosophical dimensions of cinema.

- *Talk to Her*, edited by A. W. Eaton
- *The Thin Red Line*, edited by David Davies
- *Memento*, edited by Andrew Kania
- *Eternal Sunshine of the Spotless Mind*, edited by Christopher Grau
- *Fight Club*, edited by Thomas Wartenberg
- *Vertigo*, edited by Katalin Makkai
- *Mulholland Drive*, edited by Zina Giannopoulou
- *Blade Runner*, edited by Amy Coplan and David Davies

Blade Runner

Edited by

Amy Coplan and David Davies

LONDON AND NEW YORK

First published 2015
by Routledge
2 Park Square, Milton Park, Abingdon, Oxon, OX14 4RN

and by Routledge
711 Third Ave., New York City, NY. 10017

Routledge is an imprint of the Taylor & Francis Group, an informa business

British Library Cataloguing in Publication Data
A catalogue record for this book is available from the British Library

Library of Congress Cataloging in Publication Data
Blade runner / edited by Amy Coplan and David Davies.
pages cm – (Philosophers on film)
Includes bibliographical references and index.
1. Blade runner (Motion picture) I. Coplan, Amy, editor. II. Davies, David, 1949– editor.
PN1997.B596B853 2015
791.43'72 – dc23
2014037279

ISBN: 978-0-415-48584-5 (hbk)
ISBN: 978-0-415-48585-2 (pbk)
ISBN: 978-0-203-10059-2 (ebk)

Typeset in Joanna
by Florence Production Ltd, Stoodleigh, Devon, UK

Printed and bound by CPI Group (UK) Ltd,
Croydon, CR0 4YY

Contents

Acknowledgments

We came to the film *Blade Runner* and our respective roles as co-editors of this collection by very different routes. In Amy's case, her interest in the film can be traced back to graduate school, when a friend insisted that she watch *Blade Runner* and predicted that she would come to consider it one of the best films ever made and one of the most deeply philosophical. His prediction came true. Ever since, she has been interested in how Ridley Scott's films explore and exemplify the relationships between form and content.

David, on the other hand, first saw the film much later when, at Amy's instigation, a group of those attending the ASA annual meetings in Los Angeles made an excursion to view the Final Cut, which had just opened at ArcLight Hollywood Cinemas (which provided ideal viewing conditions with its state-of-the-art sight and sound). Unsurprisingly given these facts, it was Amy who proposed this volume to Tony Bruce, and who initially approached the contributors. While David was one of those contributors, his work as co-editor only began last year when he came on board to assist in bringing the volume to completion. Thus, while Amy is solely responsible for the fact that the project of assembling and publishing this collection has a beginning and a middle, David can claim at least some responsibility for the fact that it also, in good Aristotelian fashion, has an end!

We would both like to thank all of the contributors for their excellent papers, and also apologize to them for the time it has taken for us to bring those contributions before the public eye. We would also like to thank Tony Bruce and Adam Johnson at Routledge for their extraordinary patience with this volume, but hope they share our opinion that the final product, even if it doesn't in any way excuse the delay, at least makes it less galling! We wish to express our gratitude to Timothy Juvshik, who prepared the index, and to Sarah Douglas, Anjula Semmens, and Petra Bryce for their very helpful advice during the editing and proofing processes. Early drafts of three of the papers in this collection were presented as part of a panel on *Blade Runner* held at the ASA Pacific Division meetings at Asilomar in California. We would like to thank the audience for their helpful comments.

Notes on contributors

Colin Allen is at Indiana University, Bloomington, where he teaches in the Cognitive Science Program and the Department of History and Philosophy of Science. He is a philosopher of science whose research spans animal cognition, the prospects for artificial moral agents, and algorithmic analysis of philosophical texts. He is co-author, with Wendell Wallach, of *Moral Machines: Teaching Robots Right from Wrong* (OUP, 2009).

Peter Atterton is Professor of Philosophy at San Diego State University. He is author of numerous articles on continental philosophy and ethics. His books include *The Continental Ethics Reader* (Routledge, 2003), *On Levinas* (Wadsworth, 2004), *Levinas and Buber: Dialogue and Difference* (Duquesne UP, 2004), *Animal Philosophy: Essential Readings in Continental Thought* (Continuum, 2004), and *Radicalizing Levinas* (SUNY, 2010).

Amy Coplan is Associate Professor and Chair of Philosophy at California State University, Fullerton. Her research interests include aesthetics (especially philosophy of film), philosophy of emotion, ancient Greek philosophy, and feminist philosophy. She has published on issues relating to empathy, emotional contagion, and emotional engagement with film and is the co-editor, with Peter Goldie, of the 2011 OUP interdisciplinary collection *Empathy: Philosophical and Psychological Perspectives*.

David Davies is Professor of Philosophy at McGill University. He is the author of *Art as Performance* (Blackwell, 2004), *Aesthetics and Literature* (Continuum, 2007), and *Philosophy of the Performing Arts* (Wiley-Blackwell, 2011), and editor of *The Thin Red Line* (Routledge, 2008). He has published widely on philosophical issues relating to film, photography, performance, music, literature, and visual art, and on issues in metaphysics, philosophy of mind, and philosophy of language.

Berys Gaut is Professor of Philosophy at the University of St Andrews, Scotland, and President of the British Society of Aesthetics. His books include *Art, Emotion and Ethics* (OUP, 2007) and *A Philosophy of Cinematic Art* (CUP, 2010), and he is co-editor of the *Routledge Companion to Aesthetics* (3rd edition, 2013). His next book will be on the philosophy of creativity.

Stephen Mulhall is Professor of Philosophy and a Tutorial Fellow of New College, Oxford. His research interests include Wittgenstein, Heidegger, Nietzsche, and Sartre; philosophy of film; and the relations between philosophy and the arts more generally. He is currently working on a third edition of his book *On Film* (2nd Edition: Routledge, 2008).

C. D. C. Reeve is Delta Kappa Epsilon Distinguished Professor of Philosophy at the University of North Carolina at Chapel Hill. He works primarily on Plato and Aristotle, but is interested in philosophy generally and has published on film and on the philosophy of sex and love. His most recent books include *Love's Confusions* (HUP, 2005), *Action, Contemplation, and Happiness: An Essay on Aristotle* (HUP, 2012), *Blindness and Reorientation: Problems in Plato's Republic* (OUP, 2012), and *Aristotle on Practical Wisdom* (HUP, 2013).

Note on the director

Ridley Scott was born in South Shields, England on November 30th, 1937. From 1954 to 1958, he attended West Hartlepool College of Art, where he specialized in still photography and graphic design. He went on to study at the Royal College of Art (RCA) in London (1958–61) and earned a degree in graphic design. His first cinematic venture was *Boy and Bicycle* (1961), which he directed and produced with his brother, Tony Scott, as the lead. In the same year he accepted a traveling scholarship in the US with the advertising agency Bob Drew Associates, and also worked for Richard Leacock and D. A. Pennebaker as an editing assistant at Time/Life Inc.

In 1962, Scott returned to the United Kingdom and became a television art director and set designer at the BBC, while also (1963) beginning to work as a television commercial art director. He took a BBC director's course and directed his first television program, *Softly Softly*, a police drama. In 1964, he also directed both *The Informer* for the BBC and his first television commercial for Gerber Products Company. He then left the BBC for a career in independent television production. In 1965, he created *Ridley Scott Associates* in London with his brother Tony as his first associate. By the early 1970s he had directed and/or produced hundreds of commercials.

The first feature film that he directed was *The Duelists* (1977), based on the story *The Duel* by Joseph Conrad. This film won Best First Work at the Cannes Film Festival. The picture that first brought him international recognition as a director, however, was *Alien* (1979), and in the same year he directed a high-profile commercial for Chanel No. 5. Scott has continued to divide his attention between feature films and commercials. The Theatrical Cut of *Blade Runner* was released in 1982, while in 1984 he directed the famous "1984" commercial for Apple/Macintosh, which aired in the USA during Super Bowl XVIII. Subsequently, Scott has directed a broad range of films in different genres: *Legend* (a medieval fantasy released in 1985 in Europe, and in 1986 in North America), *Someone to Watch Over Me* (a thriller, 1987), *Black Rain* (a police thriller, 1989), *Thelma and Louise* (a road movie about two women who become outlaws, 1991), *1492: Conquest of Paradise* (a historical epic, 1992), *White Squall* (an adventure film, 1996), *G. I. Jane* (an action movie, 1997), *Gladiator* (a historical epic, 2000), *Hannibal* (a sequel to Jonathan Demme's *Silence of the Lambs*, 2001), *Black Hawk Down* (based on Mark Bowden's book about a helicopter crash that left a group of American soldiers stranded in Somalia, 2002), *Matchstick Men* (a comedy based on a novel by Eric Garcia, 2003), *Kingdom of Heaven* (a historical epic about the Crusades, 2005), *A Good Year* (a romantic comedy-drama based on a book by Peter Maylem, 2006), *American Gangster* (a crime drama, 2007), *Body of Lies* (a spy film, 2008), *Robin Hood* (an action adventure drama, 2010), *Prometheus* (science fiction, not a direct prequel to *Alien* but said to take place in the same universe as the *Alien* films, 2012), and *The Counselor* (a thriller based on a screenplay by Cormac McCarthy, 2013). A 'Director's Cut' of *Blade Runner* was released in 1992, and Scott oversaw the creation of a 'Final Cut' that was released in 2007.

Scott has also been involved in the production of a broad range of other films, television shows, and made-for-tv movies through his motion picture and television production company, founded in 1980 as *Percy Main Productions* but renamed *Scott Free Productions* in 1984. In 1986, *Ridley Scott Associates*, which specializes in film and television advertising commercials, opened offices in Los Angeles and New York.

Scott has received three Oscar nominations for Best Director, for *Thelma and Louise* (1992), *Gladiator* (2001), and *Black Hawk Down* (2003). *Gladiator* won the Oscar for Best Picture (2001). In 2003, he was knighted by Queen Elizabeth II for his contribution to the British film industry.

List of characters and cast

In alphabetical order (by character name)

Roy Batty	(Rutger Hauer)
Bryant	(M. Emmet Walsh)
Hannibal Chew	(James Hong)
Rick Deckard	(Harrison Ford)
Gaff	(Edward James Olmos)
Holden	(Morgan Paull)
Leon	(Brion James)
Pris	(Daryl Hannah)
Rachael	(Sean Young)
J. F. Sebastian	(William Sanderson)
Eldon Tyrell	(Joe Turkel)
Zhora	(Joanna Cassidy)

List of figures

Chapter 1

Amy Coplan and David Davies

INTRODUCTION

THE CHOICE OF RIDLEY SCOTT'S *Blade Runner* as the subject for a book in the Routledge series *Philosophers on Film* is not surprising. The mandate of the series is to look not merely at how philosophical themes can be present in cinematic works, but also at how cinema itself can function as a medium in which philosophical work can be done. The idea of "film as philosophy" has been promoted recently by a number of philosophers – Noel Carroll (2006), Stephen Mulhall (2002), and Thomas Wartenberg (2007) to name but three. And *Blade Runner* is a film that has been cited as an example of how cinema can function as a philosophical medium. Mulhall, in particular, has characterized *Blade Runner* as "explicitly concerned with what it is to be a human being" – clearly, on at least one reading, a matter for philosophical inquiry.

The papers in this collection make significant and novel contributions to the already extensive literature on the philosophical dimensions of *Blade Runner*. These contributions address both the substantive philosophical content of the film – philosophical issues about what is distinctively human, for example, which the film can be understood as exploring – and ways in which the film opens up and explores questions about the nature and values of cinema itself – philosophical issues *about* film, including the plausibility of the idea of "film as philosophy" and the kinds of cognitive values ascribable to a film like *Blade Runner*. However, before returning to these issues and offering a brief summary of the arguments of the papers in this collection, it will be helpful to place both the film and the papers in a broader context. We shall look at the history of the making of the film itself, the history of its critical reception, the influence that it has had on the development and understanding of cinema, and the different ways in which it has been interpreted by commentators.

The making of *Blade Runner*

As is widely acknowledged, the inspiration for the narrative context and characters of Scott's film came from the book *Do Androids Dream of Electric Sheep* by the science fiction writer Philip K. Dick. Much less widely recognized is that the book and the resulting film present this context and these characters very differently, in the interests of articulating sometimes strikingly contrasting thematic meanings. David Davies's contribution to this collection includes a detailed exploration of salient differences between Dick's book and Scott's film, and of their thematic significance, and the interested reader is referred to his paper. What we shall do here, however, is look at the history of the making of the film itself.

One question that arises as soon as serious conversation about *Blade Runner* begins is "which *Blade Runner?*", for there are multiple versions of the film, and the differences between them are not at all trivial. While it is not uncommon for films to be released on DVD and for digital download with technical improvements or as extended versions that incorporate additional footage, it is rare for such changes or additions to result in significantly different interpretations or to inspire the kind of controversy that surrounds the different versions of *Blade Runner*.

The five-disc *Complete Collector's Edition* that was released in 2007 includes five different versions of the film – the US Theatrical Cut (1982), the International Theatrical Cut (1982), the Director's Cut (1992), the pre-release Workprint (1982), and the Final Cut (2007). According to some sources, however, some of the pre-screenings for the US Theatrical Cut, and some screenings that took place prior to the release of the Director's Cut, showed versions of the film other than these five. There is also said to be a four-hour 'rough cut,' which was the first version of the film that Scott and others viewed. Depending on the criteria used to determine what qualifies as a distinct version of the film, there are as many as nine distinct cuts of the film.[1] But the five versions included in the 2007

Collector's Edition are regarded as the most important and will be the focus of our attention here.

The producers of *Blade Runner* began making changes to the film even before its official release to the general public. This was due to the disappointing audience reactions to the sneak previews that Warner Brothers held in Dallas, Texas, and Denver, Colorado in early March of 1982.[2] Some audience members said that they had difficulty following and understanding the plot, some found the film's ending confusing and unsatisfying, and some complained about the "dark and gloomy" character of the film.[3] In order to address these concerns, the studio required that additional voice-over narration be added, along with a different ending. This ending was created from new live-action footage of Rachael and Deckard, shot by Scott in late March, combined with shots of mountainous landscapes taken from outtakes of Stanley Kubrick's *The Shining* (1980).[4]

A new version of the film incorporating these changes was shown on May 8, 1982 at another sneak preview screening held in San Diego, CA. This was attended by several of the filmmakers and cast, including Ridley Scott, Douglas Trumbull, Joanna Cassidy, and Harrison Ford.[5] Whereas the version screened in Dallas and Denver included only minimal voice-over narration during one of the final sequences, the voice-over now extended throughout the film. The rationale for this was that it would encourage viewers to identify more with Deckard and would help make the plot and thematic content easier to understand. It appears that Scott himself played no part in the writing of the additional voice-overs, and that this was just one way in which the revised cut departed from his own original vision for the film. In addition, the film's ambiguous, more "European" ending – an elevator door shown closing in front of Rachael's and Deckard's faces – was replaced with a "happy ending" in which Rachael and Deckard escape from the city and are shown driving through a verdant landscape.[6] Audience response to the San Diego screening of this revised version was interpreted as considerably stronger than at the Denver and Dallas screenings.

Blade Runner was released nationwide in approximately 1,300 US theaters on June 25, 1982. This version is alternately referred to as the Theatrical Cut, the US Theatrical Cut, or the Domestic Cut. Though very similar to the version shown in San Diego, it is not identical. Scott deleted a few shots and reworked a few others. Nevertheless, the

Theatrical Cut preserves the Chandleresque voice-over and the "happy ending." Although these two features of the film have been highly controversial and frequently criticized by fans, critics, and some of the filmmakers, the Theatrical Cut has its defenders, including one of the contributors to this collection and some of the film's high-profile fans, such as filmmaker Guillermo del Toro.

The International Theatrical Cut – also released in 1982 – added approximately 15 seconds of extra graphic footage that, according to Sammon,[7] was cut from the Theatrical Cut after the Dallas/Denver screenings. As a result, certain scenes were more violent. When Roy murders Tyrell, there is a close-up of Roy sinking his thumbs into Tyrell's eyes, which are then shown bleeding. Also added to this scene is a close-up of Roy removing his thumbs from Tyrell's eyes. There are additional shots during the fight between Deckard and Pris. Finally, in the rooftop scene with Deckard and Roy, when Roy pierces his hand with the nail, there are additional shots of the nail penetrating his skin.

As just noted, the Theatrical Cut departed in significant ways from Scott's vision for the film because of commercially motivated interventions by the studio.[8] The rediscovery of the Workprint may have played an important part in the decision to create a version that reversed the artistic impact of these interventions.[9] Thus on September 11, 1992, a little over ten years after *Blade Runner*'s initial release, a new version of the film – the Director's Cut – was released to 58 theaters around the US.

This version of the film includes some highly significant and controversial changes that are still the subject of lively debate. The voice-over added right before the official release of the Theatrical Cut is gone, as is the "happy ending." In the Director's Cut, Deckard no longer narrates the story for viewers, and the ending is more ambiguous. As in the original "European" ending, we watch as elevator doors close on Rachael and Deckard and are left uncertain what will become of them, how long they will live, and if they will escape from the city. Although these differences are highly important, the change that created the most debate is the addition of the now-famous unicorn sequence.[10, 11]

In the Director's Cut, the unicorn sequence occurs during the scene in Deckard's apartment that takes place just after Rachael has fled in tears, having shown up distraught over the revelation about her identity and having now learned that her memories aren't truly her own. Deckard is shown sitting at his piano and drinking, and the image then dissolves to a 12-second shot that looks like nothing else we have seen in the film up to that point. A white unicorn in a green forest is shown in slow motion galloping right toward the camera and then shaking its head and mane. We immediately cut back to Deckard who is still at the piano with the photographs he has been examining. Due to the timing and placement of the sequence, it's clear that the image of the unicorn is a dream, a memory, or a thought of Deckard's; it's an episode in his mental life.

This is critical because of its bearing on the meaning of the silver foil origami unicorn that Gaff leaves for Deckard at the end of the film. In the Theatrical Cut, we never see Deckard dreaming of a unicorn and thus the meaning behind Gaff's origami unicorn is ambiguous. But now that we know that Deckard has dreamt of a unicorn, a strong case can be made that Gaff leaves the unicorn to communicate to Deckard that he – Gaff – knows something about the content of Deckard's dreams. But how could Gaff know this? In the same way, it would seem, that Deckard knows about the contents of Rachael's memories: he knows because the memories were implanted and thus could be discovered by reading Rachael's file. Following the same line of reasoning, Gaff could know about Deckard's unicorn dream only if it were a function of something implanted. If this is the case, then we have very good evidence that Deckard is himself a replicant.[12] And, as many commentators, including some of the contributors to this collection, have argued, this significantly affects the thematic meaning of the film. This indeed is a principal reason why critics and viewers argue that one's interpretation of *Blade Runner* depends on the version under discussion.

Although Ridley Scott considered the Director's Cut to be an improvement on the Theatrical Cut, he was still not entirely satisfied, and in 2007 another version – the Final Cut – received a limited theatrical run and was made available on DVD. In making the Final Cut, Scott was able to draw upon a cache of original negatives unearthed in a storage facility in Burbank in around 2001 by Charles de Lauzirika, the producer of the *Collector's Edition*.[13] The major difference between the Final Cut and the Director's Cut is the markedly improved quality of the image and sound. A new digital print of the film was created from the original negatives, and the special effects were updated and polished.[14] The Vangelis soundtrack has been remastered in 5.1 Dolby Digital Surround Sound. But there are also changes and additions in content, involving extra shots and some extended sequences. New footage was shot for the scene in which Deckard chases and kills Zhora (Joanna Cassidy). In the previous versions of the film, when Zhora crashes through the glass display cases it is obvious that the person in the scene is a stunt double and not Joanna Cassidy. For the Final Cut, the scene was reshot and Joanna Cassidy performed the stunt herself. As a result, Zhora's death scene is much improved.[15] In addition, graphic shots of violence that were only in the International Theatrical Cut have been restored in the Final Cut so that Roy's killing of Tyrell is a bit more gruesome, as is Pris's fight with Deckard.

Some changes were also made to the dialogue. In the scene in which Bryant meets with Deckard and briefs him on the replicants, he now describes Leon's job. Perhaps more significantly, when he explains what happened to the replicants as they returned to Earth, he says that "*Two* of them got fried running through an electrical field." In previous versions of the film, he says "*One* of them got fried." This change addresses some confusion regarding the "6th replicant" mentioned in earlier versions.[16] Two more dialogue changes show up in the scene in which Roy confronts Tyrell. In previous versions of the film, during this confrontation Roy says to Tyrell, "I want more life, fucker." In the Final Cut, this line has been changed to "I want more life, father." A possible significance of this change is that it resonates with the idea, central to this scene, that Tyrell is Roy's creator. The second dialogue change occurs when, after killing Tyrell, Roy says, "I'm sorry Sebastian. Come, come."[17]

There have been numerous reports that a sequel or prequel to *Blade Runner* is planned, and a recent interview with Ridley Scott supports this claim. Scott (2013) states that "we're working on *Blade Runner* 2 right now – that will happen sooner or later." But, given the many other projects Scott discusses in the same interview, it may be a few years before *Blade Runner* 2 appears.

Reception and influence

The response to *Blade Runner* among critics, audiences, and academics has been deeply divided, and yet its influence is unquestionable. Will Brooker points out that by 2003 "*Blade Runner* became a verb."[18] Citing William Gibson's description of Tokyo as having been "Blade Runnered," Brooker writes: "Gibson had no need to italicize the title, or note the director's name . . . ; every reader would know what he meant and call to mind the right image."[19] In a similar vein, film critic Roger Ebert, after faulting himself for referring to replicants without explanation of the term in a discussion of the Final Cut, goes on to say that "it is a tribute to the influence and reach of *Blade Runner* that twenty-five years after its release virtually everyone reading this knows about replicants."[20] *Time Magazine*'s Richard Corliss writes that the film has matured into "one of the seminal artifacts and artworks of science fiction filmmaking."[21] Indeed, 30 years after its initial theatrical release, interest in the film endures, debates about its meaning persist, and filmgoers, science fiction fans, and theorists continue to find it relevant to and resonant with contemporary concerns.[22]

Today, *Blade Runner*'s importance is widely recognized, but it was by no means an instant classic. Early reception was decidedly mixed, with both critics and audiences split.[23] The majority of critics praised at least some formal elements of the film, especially the now-famous *mise en scène*, but many criticized the film's plot, characters, and/or its bleak dystopic vision of the future.[24, 25] Janet Maslin, for example, called the film "muddled yet mesmerizing," and argued that the narrative was a mess and that the impressive special effects ran away with the film. Nevertheless, she describes these special effects as "superb," and claims that the film is "as intricately detailed as anything a science fiction film has yet envisioned."[26] Pauline Kael wrote a long and careful review for the *New Yorker* but was harshly critical of many aspects of the film, including the development of the characters (especially Deckard), the coherence of the setting and plot, and the fact that the film, in her view, fails to engage the audience directly or to make them care about what happens to any of the characters. In spite of her unfavorable view, Kael describes the sets as "extraordinary" and argues that *Blade Runner* "has its own look," and that "a visionary sci-fi movie that has its own look can't be ignored – it has its place in film history."[27]

Although *Blade Runner* received some awards when it was released, almost all of these were for technical elements of the film rather than for its excellence overall. In the United States, it was nominated for two Academy Awards (Academy of Motion Picture Arts and Sciences): one for Visual Effects and one for Set Direction. In the United Kingdom, it was nominated for eight BAFTAs (British Academy of Film and Television Awards) and won the award for Best Cinematography, as well as the award for Best Production Design/Art Direction. The London Critics Circle gave *Blade Runner* a Special Achievement Award for Visual Concept in 1983. Many in the science fiction community were quicker to embrace the film than those in the film industry. It won the famed Hugo Award for Best Science Fiction Film of 1982.

There are interesting parallels between *Blade Runner* and another important science fiction film: *2001: A Space Odyssey* (Stanley Kubrick, 1968). Both films were inspired by works of important science fiction writers – Philip K. Dick's *Do Androids Dream of Electric Sheep* and Arthur C. Clarke's *The Sentinel*, respectively.[28] Each film initially received mixed reviews from both audiences and critics. And each film quickly developed a cult following and was eventually recognized as a significant and valuable work of art. These similarities may perhaps tell us something about how critics and audiences respond to mainstream science fiction films that are intellectually challenging and that employ new and effective cinematic techniques. They do not know what to make of such films when they first encounter them, but over time and after repeated viewings, their thoughts about the films develop and their appreciation deepens.[29]

In the years immediately following its release, and in part owing to its availability on home video and laser disc and multiple runs on cable television and even prime time television in the US and Japan, *Blade Runner* quickly achieved its cult status and attracted a devoted, if not obsessive, fan base along with the attention of cultural critics and academic theorists from a range of disciplines.[30] Thus, even though *Blade Runner* was neither a box-office nor a critical success right away, it would, like *2001: A Space Odyssey*, become one of the most important films of the late twentieth century. *Blade Runner*'s fan community continues to grow today and remains active through websites; discussion boards; niche groups focusing on specific elements of the film such as props or screenings; and participation in film festivals. There are also numerous articles and at least one book devoted to *Blade Runner*'s cult status and fandom activity.[31]

Blade Runner's growing success was not simply a result of the film's finding a wider audience, though this almost certainly played a role. Major critics and audience members changed their minds about it, which is something that rarely happens, particularly among film critics.[32] In the featurette "The Nexus Generation: Fans and Filmmakers," included on Disc 4 of the *Collector's Edition*, *LA Times* film critic Kenneth Turan describes his shifting view: "I can't say I knew immediately that this was a masterpiece. I did not . . . I thought it was an interesting film. I thought it was a strong film. I thought the visuals were amazing, but the voice-over really bothered me and it didn't make me think that this was a film for the ages, *but I changed my mind*." Roger Ebert, arguably the most famous film critic in the US, also revised his view:

> This is a seminal film, building on older classics like 'Metropolis' (1926) or 'Things to Come,' but establishing a pervasive view of the future that has influenced science fiction films ever since . . . I have never quite embraced 'Blade Runner,' admiring it at arm's length, but now it's time to cave in and admit it to the canon . . . Ridley Scott is a considerable director who makes no small plans . . . He has the gift of making action on a vast scale seem comprehensible. I have been assured that my problems in the past with 'Blade Runner' represent a failure of my own taste and imagination.[33]

For both Turan and Ebert, appreciation for *Blade Runner* appears to have developed over time and through repeated viewings. This was also the case for the filmmaker Frank Darabont, who went from feeling ambivalent about the film to becoming a diehard fan. In the featurette on the *Collector's Edition* DVD – "The Nexus Generation: Fans and Filmmakers" – he ventures an explanation of the change in his view:

> The very first time I saw it I was a little ambivalent about it. I've asked myself what is it about the movie that kept me at a distance the first time and I think that my answer would have to be this. The brilliance of what Ridley did with the scale of it and the production design of it disguised the fact that there was a very compelling story there . . . And it wasn't until the movie started to show on cable, probably by the third time I'd seen it, that that ambivalence had just blossomed into this passionate love of the film.

Darabont is one on a long list of filmmakers who cite *Blade Runner* and Ridley Scott as significant influences. Others include Christopher Nolan, Guillermo Del Toro, Lana and Andy Wachowski, Mark Romanek, Ronald Moore, Joseph Kahn, Joe Carnahan, Steve Loter, and Jeff Cronenweth.[34]

Del Toro, for example, likens *Blade Runner* to a cinematic drug, and says that after he watched it his life was changed. Mark Romanek says that he saw the movie and wanted to live there in that world, and that afterward he started decorating and lighting his apartment to make it look more like *Blade Runner*. Christopher Nolan, when talking about *Blade Runner* as an influence on his *Dark Knight* trilogy, says it is "simply the most memorable evocation of all that is spectacular and oppressive about the city." And Jeff Cronenweth comments on the film as follows: "It was so different. It wasn't *Star Wars*. It wasn't *E.T.*. It wasn't anything that we really had seen like that. And I was just taken aback, blown away."[35]

It would be difficult to overstate the influence that *Blade Runner* has had on film, television, and popular culture in general. It is a watershed film that established a new precedent in both the look and vision of science fiction film. As many commentators have remarked, prior to *Blade Runner*, science fiction films were usually brightly lit and featured a utopian vision of the future. *Blade Runner* led us into the dark. Ridley Scott, in collaboration with Douglas Trumbull, "visual futurist" Syd Mead, David Dryer, Richard Yuricich, Lawrence G. Paull, and others who worked on the film, created a megalopolis that looked like nothing that had been seen on film before and that would alter the way we imagine the future.

Blade Runner's impact can be seen in countless films, including but not limited to *Brazil* (Terry Gilliam, 1985), *Ghost in the Shell* (Mamoru Oshii, 1995), *Judge Dredd* (Danny Cannon, 1995), *Strange Days* (Kathryn Bigelow, 1995), *The Fifth Element* (Luc Besson, 1997), *Gattaca* (Andrew Niccol, 1997), *Dark City* (Alex Proyas, 1998) *The Matrix* (Andy and Lana Wachowski, identified as the Wachowski Brothers, 1999), *Minority Report* (Steven Spielberg, 2002), *Renaissance* (Christian Volckman, 2005), *Batman Begins* (Christopher Nolan, 2005), *The Dark Knight* (Christopher Nolan, 2008), and *The Dark Knight Rises* (Christopher Nolan, 2012). Television shows clearly influenced by *Blade Runner* include *Max Headroom* (1987–8), *Battlestar Galactica* (2004–9), and *Almost Human* (2013).

Another way in which *Blade Runner* has been influential is through the cyberpunk movement, with which it is closely associated. Cyberpunk refers to a literary movement that emerged within science fiction in America in the 1980s. It develops a new approach to the importance of technology and its ever-increasing role in contemporary experience, and combines features of hi-tech and popular culture. Cyberpunk stories often incorporate the aesthetic of *film noir* and elements of detective fiction, and typically take place on Earth in a bleak, dystopian near-future that is highly technological and is governed by corporate entities. Cyberpunk protagonists are usually marginalized individuals who rebel against society and often reshape the tools of the rich and powerful to subvert corporatization and mass conformity. More than perhaps any other film, *Blade Runner* exemplifies the look and style of cyberpunk. William Gibson, one of the pioneers of the cyberpunk movement, saw *Blade Runner* as he was writing *Neuromancer*, his debut novel and one of the formative works of cyberpunk. In a recent interview, he explains its effect on him:

> I was afraid to watch *Blade Runner* in the theater because I was afraid the movie would be better than what I myself had been able to imagine. In a way, I was right to be afraid, because even the first few minutes were better. Later, I noticed that it was a total box office flop, in first theatrical release. That worried me, too. I thought, uh-oh. He got it right and nobody cares! Over a few years, though, I started to see that in some weird way it was the most influential film of my lifetime, up to that point. It affected the way people dressed, it affected the way people decorated nightclubs. Architects started building office buildings that you could tell they had seen in *Blade Runner*. It had an astonishingly broad aesthetic impact on the world.[36]

Interpretations of *Blade Runner* and overview of the chapters

Interpretations

Cyberpunk readings are one type of interpretation of the film to be found in the critical literature. But the diversity of interpretations, and the different issues, themes, and questions that commentators have found interestingly exemplified in the film, further testify to its thematic richness. There have been a number of feminist analyses, which focus on such issues as Deckard's treatment of Rachael, Rachael's transformation in the film, and the presentation and "retirement" of Pris and Zhora, who is shot in the back.[37] Other interpretations examine the film's treatment of oppression in relation to race, class, and slavery.[38] Closely related and often overlapping with these are some interpretations that explore the themes of capitalism and corporate control,[39] or that focus on ways in which *Blade Runner* illuminates the meanings of the city, urbanization, and space.[40] In addition to these topics, commentators have also developed interpretations of the film that center on the figure of the android and our relationship to technology.[41] Still others have concentrated on the film's exploration of perception and its limitations, particularly in regard to vision, eyes, and different ways of seeing.[42] Much has also been written on *Blade Runner* as science fiction and/or as a postmodern film.[43] And this survey of types of interpretations is by no means exhaustive!

A number of philosophers who have written on the film, however, have focused on a nexus of issues relating to human nature and human capacities such as empathy, memory, and selfhood. For such philosophers, reflection on the situation of the film's replicants illuminates, both through comparison and contrast, what it is to be human. As we shall see, it is these approaches to the film that resonate most closely with the substantive topics explored by the authors in this collection. The most developed account of this kind is in Mulhall (2007). *Blade Runner*, Mulhall argues, is concerned with the essentially embodied nature of human beings and of their subsequent capacity for pain and openness to mortality. It is these qualities, shared by the replicants, that allow the latter's condition to illuminate our own. Mulhall further argues that "humanity," whether of humans or of replicants, requires acknowledgment by others, and – anticipating a theme explored in different ways in papers in this collection – that authenticity in a life is measured in terms of the intensity with which it is lived. Judith Barad (2007) offers a Sartrean analysis of *Blade Runner* that explores how, in murdering Tyrell, Roy acquires the very ability we might take to distinguish humans from the most complex of computers – the ability to live authentically and take responsibility for our own free actions. This change in Roy again serves to illuminate our own condition. Deborah Knight and George McKnight (2008), again anticipating a theme further explored in different ways in the current collection, argue that it is the distinctively emotional aspects of memory that are central to our "humanity" and to human agency.

The themes of the papers in this collection

In his contribution to this collection, Berys Gaut identifies what he takes to be the three principal philosophical themes in the film – death, empathy, and what it is to be human. As the following summaries will indicate, narrative and conceptual relationships between these themes are explored by a number of the contributors to this collection, as are connections between these themes and both memory and emotion. A second philosophical thread, however, runs through many of the papers – namely, ways in which *Blade Runner* enlarges our understanding of the cinematic medium itself and its cognitive and affective values. Gaut, Atterton, and Davies all comment directly on whether the philosophical dimensions of *Blade Runner* support the "film as philosophy" thesis. While all ascribe cognitive value to the film, they stress how it is through its affective power that cinema has such value. Coplan focuses more directly on the specific techniques and resources through which cinematic affect is produced and can thereby serve such cognitive purposes, while Mulhall continues his exploration, begun in Mulhall (2007), of ways in which *Blade Runner* comments upon the material basis of cinema and its capacity to reveal the world to us.[44]

Berys Gaut identifies three interconnected philosophical themes in *Blade Runner*: death, empathy, and what it is to be human. He argues that the film offers rich and insightful suggestions as to how these themes are interconnected, and that the manner in which this is accomplished in the film is crucial to its aesthetic and emotional power. He further argues that this illustrates the kinds of cognitive values that can be realized cinematically, but does not support the idea of film as itself a philosophical medium.

Gaut begins by highlighting the many features of *Blade Runner* that make it a "dark and death-obsessed film," something commentators have generally missed. By attending closely to these features, we come to the realization that the replicants' problem with death – most vividly expressed in Roy's dialogue with Tyrell – is simply an extreme version of our own situation. The film invites us to reflect upon this situation, that is, upon our own mortality. This is why, for Gaut, *Blade Runner* is an elegy both for the replicants and for us.

Critical attention, however, has focused on the importance of empathy for our understanding of what it is to be human. But, Gaut argues, we must carefully distinguish between two senses of humanity if we are to properly understand the bearing of empathy on being human and on Deckard's much remarked "discovery of his humanity" through his interactions with Rachael and the fugitive replicants. The latter seems incoherent if humanity is taken in a biological sense, given that the closing scene of the Director's and Final Cuts leaves no doubt that Deckard is himself a replicant, and that many biological humans in the film seem to lack empathy. We must therefore distinguish biological humanity from what Gaut terms "evaluative" humanity. In the evaluative sense, to be human means "to be disposed to kindness, forgiveness, and in general to be empathetic." Thus replicants can be evaluatively human, although not biologically human, since they can have or develop the relevant dispositions and capacity for empathy.

Gaut argues that an even more important issue that the film raises about empathy concerns the sorts of beings that feel empathy. Here the film proposes an intimate relationship between empathy and awareness of mortality, so that empathy is most powerfully evoked in relation to death. This relationship permeates the film, but is explored most notably in the character of Roy, who is shown to be a ruthless killer but who is also capable of empathy, saving Deckard from certain death. Framing this transformation in Roy is religious imagery, especially during the climactic scene in which, after chasing Deckard, Roy then saves Deckard's life. Gaut argues that death plays a critical role in Roy's empathetic action toward Deckard. Roy comes to the realization that he and Deckard are alike in the terror they experience in facing imminent death. And death is well suited to evoke empathy, Gaut claims, because it is a universal aspect of life that typically evokes powerful emotions. Indeed, it is Roy's own death after saving Deckard that first elicits in the viewer empathetic feelings towards him. Death also creates a strong need for empathetic engagement with another so that our emotional lives are shared and thus passed on, in at least some sense.

In the final section of his chapter, Gaut situates *Blade Runner* in the context of the contemporary debate over whether or not films can "do philosophy." He accepts that films can have cognitive functions and can achieve some of the same ends as philosophy, but points out that this doesn't mean that films are forms of philosophy. In addition, films typically seek to move us emotionally and aesthetically while philosophy rarely does. This point is especially relevant in the case of *Blade Runner*, which Gaut describes as "one of the most visually dense and strikingly beautiful films ever created." Reflecting upon the artistic elements of the film, Gaut argues that its cognitive vision is realized through its beauty, which he characterizes as "beauty of evanescence, decay, and death."

Peter Atterton, like Gaut, identifies death as a central thematic preoccupation of *Blade Runner*. He also agrees that this thematic preoccupation is most clearly expressed in the scene at the end of the film where Roy saves Deckard before himself dying. But Atterton locates this thematic concern in a very different philosophical tradition and accords it a correspondingly different significance. He focuses initially upon the Tyrell Corporation's boast that its replicants are "more human than human," and asks in what the humanity, and the *superior* humanity, of the replicants consists. In response to the first question, Atterton maintains that the defining human quality that the replicants share with their human counterparts is the knowledge of the certainty of their own death, and thus the need to live in a way that either affirms or denies this knowledge. This defining human quality, while it has a long philosophical and literary heritage, is best exemplified in recent philosophy by Heidegger's notion of being-toward-death as one of the existential conditions of *Dasein*. It is in sharing this defining aspect of the human condition that the replicants share in our humanity, and, indeed, share it in a more extreme form, as Gaut also notes, given their pre-determined "termination" dates.

In addressing the question as to the superior humanity of the replicants, Atterton notes first that, for Heidegger, it is crucial that *Dasein* confront its being-toward-death because only through this can we live in a way informed by an awareness of the importance, fragility, and very limited nature of our lives, and of the consequent need to realize our possibilities as fully as possible. What Heidegger terms "authentic" *Dasein* – *Dasein* that lives in full acknowledgment of its being-toward-death – is connected by Atterton to Nietzsche's "Overman," who also says "yes" to life. This kind of full authenticity in acknowledging *Dasein's* being-toward-death is exemplified in literature in such figures as Marlowe's Faust and Milton's Satan. It is exemplified in the film by Roy Batty, who contrasts strikingly with those human characters such as J. F. Sebastian who live inauthentically. Roy, though "merely" an android, represents the full potential of humanity better than any human.

Atterton maintains that it is only when we see Roy in these terms that we can understand why he saves Deckard and how, in so doing, he manifests so clearly authentic humanity. The question that Roy faces at this point is Tolstoy's question: whether there is any meaning in one's individual life that is not destroyed or devalued by one's death. In saving Deckard, he recognizes one whose own death can be postponed by his action. In so doing, he shows that the value that can survive an individual's death is the value of those surviving things that the individual has invested with value through his or her actions. Roy's subsequent death, then, "discloses truly human possibilities, which include not only a joyful celebration of life, a great 'yes' to life and concomitant 'no' to death, but also the distinctly human possibility of salvaging a meaning from life that impending death cannot efface."

Like Gaut and Davies, Atterton raises in the final sections of his paper questions about the philosophical value of a film like *Blade Runner*. He takes himself to have made manifest the unabashedly philosophical preoccupations of the film and its questioning of our ordinary conceptions of what is distinctively human. However, Atterton argues, the greatness of *Blade Runner* resides in the ways in which it goes beyond philosophical treatments of these matters and provides a dramatic illustration of the difference between "the world of lifeless mechanism in which most humans left on earth are at home, and a conception of nature as something not essentially inert or robotic, but fruitful and capable of finding a meaning in life despite the inevitable death that awaits." Atterton, then, while more favorable to the idea of "film as philosophy" than Gaut, shares with him (and with Davies) the belief that we miss the cognitive importance of a film like *Blade Runner* if we think of it as "doing philosophy," whether the latter is understood in traditionally analytic or traditionally continental terms.

C. D. C. Reeve also explores various ways in which the replicants in *Blade Runner* resemble and differ from humans. In so doing he brings out some central ambiguities in the film that call into question our natural reading of it as a romance. He first notes the crucial role ascribed to memory (see Allen's and Davies's papers for related reflections). Implanted memories ("quasi-memories") in Rachael play, for her, the same roles that real memories play for us. They give us a sense of who we are and of our place in the world, and provide "a sense of home and family, of being loved and cherished, and the sense of self that comes with it." If all of the replicants have such quasi-memories (but see Davies's paper for questions about this assumption), this explains why photographs are so precious to Leon and Rachael, and why the replicants risk returning to Earth.

Reeve argues, however, that such quasi-memories call into question whether replicants who have them possess analogues of features traditionally associated with human souls and implicated in our sense of what is necessary to be capable of love. Roy claims to have done "morally questionable things," but moral responsibility presupposes the capacity for free action and self-consciousness. That some of the replicants seem to have taken on roles other than those for which they were designed suggests that their being designed for a task is no obstacle to ascribing to them the capacities for free action and free choice that, for some philosophers, are the only ones plausibly ascribed to us: the ability to express one's "practical identity" – one's own will which reflects one's own experience and reflection. But can this apply to one such as Rachael, if her will, shaped by her quasi-memories, reflects another's experiences? The will she has may be free, but is it really *hers*? One response is to say that at least our pleasures and pains are our own. However, Reeve suggests, the problem is not thereby solved, because what gives us pleasure and pain is itself a function of our experience and reflection. It reflects, for example, our relationships with our parents. But in Rachael's case her memories of her parents are not "hers" but those of Tyrell's niece. If the "deep structure" of our style of loving is "ours" in virtue of being formed by our experiences, can even Rachael's emotional and affective responses be "hers," given that her memories are quasi-memories? The capacity for love, like the capacity for empathy, Reeve suggests, depends upon psychological processes of which we are not conscious – this is what the Voight-Kampff test measures. Rachael's failure to pass this test therefore calls into question whether she really has the capacity for love and empathy – or, rather, whether the capacities she may manifest in her behavior are really "hers." Our natural, "romantic" reading of the film is thereby rendered problematic. Reeve also asks whether we should share the idea that only that which lacks transience has value – the value that, in the human case, is supposed to be guaranteed by our immortal souls.

At the end of his paper, Reeve distinguishes two questions about the significance of the origami unicorn figure that Gaff leaves at Deckard's door at the very end of the later cuts of the film. On the standard reading, Gaff's purpose is to convey to Deckard that Deckard is a replicant. The figure communicates this to the audience as well as to Deckard because, as shown earlier in the film, Deckard has had imaginings about a unicorn. Only if Gaff had seen details of implanted memories in Deckard's "file," just as Deckard had seen such details in Rachael's "file," could Gaff have such knowledge of Deckard's inner life. Reeve doesn't dispute that the unicorn may play the role, in the cinematic narrative, of communicating Deckard's replicant status to the viewer. He argues, however, that it doesn't follow that this is Gaff's intention in leaving the unicorn figure. For we must also ask why it is the figure of a *unicorn* that he leaves. Drawing on the traditional symbolic significance of the unicorn, Reeve suggests that Gaff's message is a more personal one that acknowledges that Deckard has acted as a man, not only in his struggle with Roy but also in falling in love with, and putting himself at risk to protect, Rachael.

In his chapter "Do humans dream of emotional machines?," **Colin Allen** focuses primarily on how *Blade Runner* gets us to think philosophically about what it is to be human and on the role of emotions in our mental make-up. He claims that, while *Blade Runner* may have only in very general respects predicted subsequent developments in robotics – it "gets almost nothing right about the actual technology of robot and android development as of 2015" – and while the film's psychology is largely fictional, it still raises important questions in philosophy of mind and philosophy of cognitive science about the relationship between emotion and cognition, the nature of ethical decision-making, how developmental constraints affect the mind, and the extent to which cognitive and emotional development depend on relationships to others. The film serves as a launch pad for philosophical reflection on these questions by asking us to consider what it would be like to be a replicant, and how this might differ from what it is like to be human. The initial distinction between humans and replicants is made in terms of certain capacities for emotions, but the film remains ambiguous on how replicants and humans differ in this respect. But, Allen argues, this ambiguity may mirror the conceptual "messiness" of the issues that we may confront in reality as robotic technology develops.

To explore these questions, Allen introduces the notion of "emotional checking," which can be understood in three distinct ways. In a first sense, emotional checking is a way of verifying an individual's emotional states by reference to external signs. This is exemplified in the Voight-Kampff test – an "empathy test" designed to provoke an emotional response. Allen expresses skepticism about the scientific credibility of the Voight-Kampff test, however, in large part because of the culturally relative character of the questions posed to subjects. He contrasts this *external* checking of emotional responses with another kind of "emotional checking" that is *internal*. The interpenetration of our emotions and our memories provides us with a sense of who we are and of what matters to us, although the complexity of the relation between memory and emotion is only gestured at in the suggestion that the implanted memories in some of the Nexus 6 replicants provide a "cushion for the emotions." Such autobiographically grounded emotions provide a check that is essential for rational and ethical behavior. In many cases, such emotions influence behavior by either motivating or inhibiting action. It is in terms of this notion of emotional checking that we can explain Roy's decision not to kill Deckard. Roy's awareness of having been the author of his own life tempers his anger. (Davies's paper contains further reflections on these themes.)

The third type of emotional checking is social in nature, and reciprocal. The film explores this through its presentations of the relationships between Rachael and Deckard and between the fugitive replicants. Allen argues that, through its portrayal of love, trust, and loyalty in these relationships, the film raises philosophical questions about the ethics and psychology of trust in humans. He contends that *Blade Runner*'s depiction of the development of emotional relationships reflects an idea that cognitive science has finally begun to appreciate: that our identities and capabilities depend as much on resources outside of ourselves as they do on the brain itself. *Blade Runner* offers no definitive conclusions on this but the "emotional messiness" of the film, Allen argues, may be prophetic of the profound effects on human sensibility that may follow from the development of machines that seem, at least, to care.

While philosophical reflections upon particular films usually group disparate scenes and sequences in the interest of uncovering thematic meanings, **Stephen Mulhall** engages in a close exploration of one particular, largely overlooked, sequence in *Blade Runner*. In this sequence, Deckard uses a device called the Esper to analyze a photograph that he has recovered from Leon's apartment. Mulhall maintains that this sequence serves no obvious narrative function, but that it has a complex internal structure in virtue of which it serves both as a further articulation of the higher-level thematic content of the film and as a comment on the very nature of photography and cinema and our engagement with works in those media.

Mulhall takes the Vermeer-like qualities of Leon's photograph as an indication that Scott is interested in reflecting, in this sequence, on the distinction between painting and photography, and on the material basis of the cinematographic medium. A key factor here is the way in which the Esper-analysis sequence is experienced by the viewer: "what we know to be a computer-aided analysis of a photograph of a room is experienced quite as if we are moving around within the room itself, able to examine any portion of it." This supports Stanley Cavell's claim that, when we view a photograph, we view the objects themselves, not their representations or likenesses. While encountering something in a photograph differs from encountering it in real life, the difference is not in the nature of the things encountered. And, because our exploration of Leon's photographic image is conducted through the quasi-cinematic procedures of the Esper, what are also conveyed are truths about the material basis of cinema.

The deeper significance of the Esper-analysis sequence, however, only emerges when we register two distinct parts of this sequence. The first part, which concludes with the exploration of what is reflected in the slightly convex mirror visible through the door to the second room, conforms perfectly to the laws of geometry and physics. It also underlines how photographs differ from paintings, in that we can always ask, in the case of the former, what is going on in spaces hidden from view. In this phase of the Esper analysis, we are aware of the internal spatio-temporal coherence of the world of the film, and also of our absence from it. In the second phase of the analysis, Deckard is analyzing a second-order reflection – those things visible in the mirrored doors of the wardrobe, which are themselves reflected in the circular mirror. This set of reflections, however, does not seem to obey the laws of physics and geometry. We are no longer dealing with the kind of visual information that could be conveyed by a still photograph, however closely analyzed. Rather, the information obtained in this phase of the analysis could be attained only by actually occupying the second room, and exploiting the full reflective potential of the mirrored doors by altering one's position with respect to them. There is, then, a "sudden loss of coherence" when we move from the reflections in the circular mirror to those in the wardrobe doors. This transition can be seen as a change in viewpoint, from that of a viewer of a photograph to that of one who inhabits the room photographed.

Mulhall offers a number of suggestions as to the significance of this transition. Its narrative import is to signal how Deckard's abilities as a blade runner both depend upon and are threatened by his ability to take on the perspective of his prey. More thematically, the shift of viewpoint implicates the viewer in Deckard's realization that the replicant's perspective is one which we can share. We also see a thematic rather than a narrative significance in Deckard's Esper exploration of the scales on Zhora's dress. But the transition and the sequence in which it occurs also further Scott's attempts to get the viewer to reflect on the nature of the cinematic medium, seducing the viewer "into experiencing an impossible transgression of boundaries between representations, and between representations and what they represent." We thereby see that something's being a film doesn't prevent it from presenting us with "the full richness of human reality."

Amy Coplan examines some of the ways in which the formal elements of *Blade Runner* influence how we experience and interpret its meanings. She focuses on how the film's use of the stylistic conventions of *film noir*, moving light, and an extremely detailed environment and atmosphere expresses and elicits mood responses in viewers, thereby influencing how they engage with and interpret the film. While many commentators have discussed the physical world of the film – "the dark urban future of a polluted, oversaturated megalopolis with neon lights, monolithic buildings, gigantic animated billboards, congested air space, streets teeming with people and activities, and layers upon layers of visual and aural complexity" – Coplan focuses upon the cinematographic devices employed in presenting that environment to the viewer. She argues that the resulting formal elements lead viewers to adopt an active stance in watching the film by creating an ominous mood of paranoia and uncertainty. This supports the idea that "the way films make us feel plays a fundamental role in what and how they make us think."

Coplan begins by sketching contemporary scientific work on mood. She characterizes a mood as "an affective state involving physiological arousal and usually distinctive phenomenological feelings," and discusses the distinctions between moods and emotions. Mood can affect other cognitive states and processes in various ways. A mood raises or lowers an individual's susceptibility to certain emotions, renders certain kinds of memories more or less accessible, and bears more generally upon cognitive processing and mental flexibility. Coplan then endorses the claim that it is mood, rather than details of setting or narrative content, that is distinctive of *film noir*, and outlines the kinds of cinematographic and other devices whereby the "mood" of a *noir* film is established. *Noir* films typically convey "feelings of paranoia, instability, insecurity, and alienation. They present us with a world that is full of decay, pollution, rain, and darkness, and in which many of the characters are haunted by some unseen threat." *Blade Runner* fuses these traditional elements of *noir* cinema with generic features of science fiction, initiating the idea of a "neo *noir*" or "future *noir*" cinema.

In the remainder of her paper, Coplan explores how formal elements of *Blade Runner* generate a mood of *noir* and thereby crucially inflect the viewer's experience. She focuses on ways in which the film's cinematographer, Jordan Cronenweth, makes use of light, a traditional *noir* device. Two distinctive features of the film are the dominant use of backlighting, and the use of carefully projected shafts of light. Coplan examines examples of each of these features and analyzes their affective force. "By lighting shots and scenes for strong affective impact," she argues, "Cronenweth and Scott cause the environment and the light in the story to shape the way we go on to watch and interpret the meaning of the film." The most extended analysis of the use of lighting techniques for *noir* effects is of the scene where Deckard first encounters Rachael and Tyrell at the Tyrell Corporation building. Coplan concludes by examining ways in which Cronenweth makes use, for affective purposes, of moving light sources in the film.

David Davies addresses three distinct issues, some also addressed by other authors in the collection, and argues that they are connected in interesting ways. He begins by drawing attention to striking differences, both in detail and in thematic meaning, between *Blade Runner* and the literary work by Philip K. Dick upon which it is in some sense based. In comparing and contrasting the two works, he asks whether differences in medium have any bearing on the kinds of cognitive value that artworks can have, and, more especially, on their ability to function as thought experiments. He examines some possible sources of incoherence in the narrative of *Blade Runner* which might call into question its validity as a thought experiment. In exploring one possible source of incoherence, he argues, like Gaut and Allen, that implanted memories, and memories more generally, play a crucial role in the "humanity" of the replicants.

Davies then argues that *Blade Runner* is not plausibly read as a thought experiment, even if Dick's novel does lend itself to such a reading. He suggests, in line with Gaut and Atterton, that the film can nonetheless be ascribed significant cognitive value in virtue of its powerful experiential, and especially affective, impact upon the receiver.

In surveying differences between the narratives of Dick's book and Scott's film, Davies notes in particular the different ways in which the replicants are portrayed. He argues that, as a result, the narratives articulate very different and potentially conflicting thematic meanings. Borrowing Gaut's distinction between "biological" and "evaluative" senses of humanity, Davies argues that, while Dick's narrative is intended to point to the possibility of biological humanity in the absence of evaluative humanity, Scott's narrative concern is with the possibility of evaluative humanity in the absence of biological humanity. He also notes that, as viewers, we are led to affirm the latter not only because of how the replicants in general are portrayed, but also because we identify with Deckard, through whose eyes we see much of the drama unfold. When we realize that Deckard is himself a replicant, this doesn't affect our empathetic engagement with him because by this point we are already convinced of his evaluative humanity.

Davies then examines possible sources of incoherence in Scott's narrative so construed. A serious lacuna is that we are offered no obvious explanation as to how Rachael and Roy can possess the capacities for empathy and moral action that they manifest if they lack biological humanity. Davies argues that these capacities can be understood as a function of memory, and that we can understand in these terms both the way in which implanted memories can serve as "a cushion for the emotions" and how both real and implanted memories can provide a basis, independent of biology, for both empathy and moral action. This allows us to understand the significance of Roy's dwelling on his memories in his dying speech.

Having canvassed the possibility that both book and film are intended to function as thought experiments for their respective thematic conclusions, Davies then argues against such a reading of the film. He first surveys some of the recent literature on "film as philosophy" that examines whether films can serve as thought experiments for philosophical conclusions. He then argues that, while this may indeed be possible, *Blade Runner* is not usefully seen in this way. This is in part because the persuasiveness of the thematic meaning of the film relies upon the very empathetic tendencies in the viewer that the film, if viewed as a thought experiment, would be intended to validate. As Davies puts this difficulty, "how can our natural responses show that our natural responses are justified?" But he agrees with Atterton and Gaut that this doesn't diminish the cognitive value of the film. Drawing on Richard Moran's distinction between hypothetical and dramatic forms of imagining, he maintains that, while thought experiments require hypothetical imagining, a film like *Blade Runner* promotes dramatic imagining that can deepen our understanding of philosophical issues and place our intuitive responses to them on a firmer rational foundation. Artistic cognitivism with respect to literature and cinema, then, is compatible with the acknowledgment that they may differ in their cognitive potential.

Notes

1 For a detailed explanation of the different versions of the film, including those released in various formats for home viewing – such as the Criterion Collection laser disc – see Sammon (1993; 2007a, especially 286–374); Lucas (1993); Kolb (1997); and Turan (1992).
2 Paul Sammon (1996, 286–90) reports that the marketing research team at Warner Brothers analyzed the audience reaction cards and identified five areas of criticism: difficult to understand; excessively violent; too slow; too grim; and unsatisfying in its ending.
3 Sammon (2007a, 289).
4 There is considerable controversy and conflicting reports about the origin of the voice-over narration, the recordings, and the feelings and opinions of the different parties involved. See Sammon (1996, 291–9).
5 Sammon (2007a, 304ff) discusses the possibility that Ford's presence may have made the audience reaction more favorable to the version shown, and reports that several audience reaction cards mentioned Ford's presence in the theater.
6 See Sammon (2007a, 299–308) and Kolb (1997). For the description of the original ending as "European," see the quote from Scott in Sammon (2007a, 307): "We had originally ended *Blade Runner* with what we apprehended as an ambiguous finale; European, if you will."
7 (2007a, 326).
8 For Scott's own reflections on this, see his remarks in one of his interviews with Paul Sammon quoted on p. 484 of Sammon (2007a).

9 See Kolb (1997); Sammon (2007a, 330–55; 1993); and Turan (1992).

10 The unicorn sequence is controversial because, as noted below, it is widely taken to entail that Deckard is himself a replicant. This possibility is the subject of "Deck-a-Rep?", one of the featurettes on the *Collector's Edition* DVD. In their papers in this volume both Davies and Gaut quote from "Deck-a-Rep?" Scott's remark that, given the added unicorn sequence, Deckard's replicant status is so obvious from Gaff's gesture at the end of the film that "if you don't get it you're a moron"! Scott also comments on this in one of the interviews with Paul Sammon contained in Appendix A of Sammon (2007a) – see, for example, pp. 482–3. For other views on this matter, see Nathan (2007, 65), and an interview (Ford 2007) where Harrison Ford comments: "I've said this many times, but I thought it was a mistake to suggest that Deckard was a replicant. A great mistake. Because it left the audience with no-one to root for" (quote on p. 80). David Peoples, who completed the screenplay for *Blade Runner* after creative differences with Scott led to the departure of the original screenwriter Hampton Fancher, has said (Sammon 2007a, 351–62) that he meant for the issue of Deckard's identity to be ambiguous: "In my script, it was much more ambiguous whether Ford was a replicant or not . . . I wanted people to only think as an afterthought that *maybe* Deckard was an android. I fought very hard for that. But when I finally caught the film and saw how Ridley had made the replicants' eyes glow, and then you saw Ford's eyes glow, I thought, 'Aw, shit.' That device made explicit what I'd wanted to be ambivalent."

11 Other changes were also made to the Director's Cut. For example, the soundtrack was remixed, and some dialogue was added to one of the advertisements in order to fill a gap that was left by the elimination of the voice-over. For more on these changes and the development of the Director's Cut, see Sammon (1993; 2007a, 349–59); Galagher (2002); and Bukatman (2012).

12 See Reeve's paper in this collection, however, for an alternative interpretation of Gaff's meaning.

13 This is discussed on pp. 70–2 of Paul Sammon (2007b).

14 John Howell (2007) reports that a new digital print of the film was created from the original negatives. In addition, the special effects footage was scanned in at 8,000 lines per frame, which is four times the resolution used in most restorations. See also Fischer (2007).

15 For more on the reshoot, see Paul Sammon (2007b). He interviewed Charles De Lauzirika, who discusses the processes used to fix the scene as well as Cassidy's ability to successfully mimic the movements she made years ago and that "she looks exactly like she did while she was making *Blade Runner*" (72).

16 Scott intended to have one more replicant in the film, a female named Mary (Stacey Nelkin), but her part was cut due to budget constraints. According to Scott, this is why Bryant mentioned six replicants. See Appendix A of Sammon (2007a, 487).

17 There are some other minor changes, as well, which are discussed by Howell (2007) and De Lauzirika in Sammon (2007b). These include an added shot of the exotic dancers in hockey masks, an added shot of a crowded street, and the trimming of some scenes due to a lag that resulted after the removal of the voice-over.

18 Brooker (2005b), pp. 1–10. The quote is on p. 1.

19 Ibid. Gibson uses the term "Blade Runner" as a verb in his 2003.

20 Roger Ebert, *Blade Runner: The Final Cut* in his 2010, p. 76.

21 Richard Corliss (2012).

22 See, for example, Norris (2013); Hills (2005; 2011); Brooker (2005a; 2005b); Barlow (2005); and Kerman (2005).

23 For a discussion of audience response, see Sammon (2007a, 286–90).

24 For more on the critical and popular reception of the film, see Kolb (1990; 1997); Sammon (2007a, 313–15 and 368–9); Bukatman (2012); Gray (2005); Brooker (2005a; 2005b); and Hills (2011).

25 Other elements of the film about which opinions differed greatly included the Vangelis soundtrack, Scott's synthesis of science fiction and *film noir*, the performances of the actors, the relationship of the film to its plot, the relationship of the film to Dick's novel, and the moral, social, and political dimensions of the film.

26 Janet Maslin (1982).

27 Pauline Kael (1984).

28 Clarke wrote the novel 2001: *A Space Odyssey* as the film was being made; it was published soon after the film was released.

29 In his *Empire* interview with Paul Sammon, Scott (2007) speculates as to the possible reasons for the initially lukewarm reception that the film received. He cites three factors: 1) people were expecting something very different, in part due to the casting of Harrison Ford, whom audiences knew from *Star Wars* and *Raiders of the Lost Ark*. They were therefore unprepared for the darkness of the film – both the darkness of the thematic content and its vision of the future, and the literal darkness of a film that came to be identified as "future noir." 2) Relatedly, *Blade Runner* was released during the same summer as E.T. Given the latter's fairy-tale qualities and "happy ending," the response to *Blade Runner* might represent a preference on the part of audiences and critics for a happy, positive view of the world over the dark and depressing cyberpunk view of *Blade Runner*. 3) The degree of visual and aural information presented by the film and the details and complexity of its world may have overwhelmed people, distracting them from the story and making it difficult for them to follow the narrative threads – a view shared by many other commentators.

30 Paul Sammon discusses the importance of the film's release on home video and laser disc, which was extremely successful. He argues that it played a critical role in increasing the film's fan base (2007a, 322–5).

31 The book-length treatment is Matt Hills' *Blade Runner: Cultographies* (2011), which was published as part of Wallflower's new *Cultographies* series, which features individual studies of cult films.
32 While it may be tempting to assume that the shift in people's reaction to the film was caused by the release of the Director's Cut, there's reason to doubt this explanation. William Kolb (1997) reports that the critical reaction to the Director's Cut was largely unchanged from the reaction to the initial theatrical release. The same was not the case, however, with audience responses.
33 Ebert (2010, 77, 79).
34 Jeff Cronenweth's father, Jordan Cronenweth, was the award-winning cinematographer who shot *Blade Runner*.
35 The quotations from Del Toro, Romanek, and Cronenweth are also from the featurette "The Nexus Generation." For the Nolan quotation, see J. Vejvoda (2012).
36 Gibson (2011).
37 See, for example, Barr (1997); Jermyn (2005); and Wood (2003, 161–7).
38 See, for example, Desser (1997); Redmond (2005); Alessio (2005); and Yu (2008).
39 A particularly rich and interesting interpretation of this type is Kellner, Liebowitz, and Ryan (1984). The authors argue that *Blade Runner* presents an ideologically ambivalent dystopia that reveals conflicts existing in advanced capitalist societies. The images of the film, they maintain, suggest "the incongruity of late capitalism" and thereby articulate fears of capitalist exploitation, technological dehumanization, and the collapse of values like love, empathy, and community.
40 See, for example, Sobchack (1997) and Bukatman (1997; 2012).
41 Colin Allen's paper in this collection touches upon these themes.
42 See, for example, Bukatman (2012).
43 Ibid. See also Sobchack (1997); Milner (2004); and Yu (2008).
44 For a very different "psychoanalytic" reading of how *Blade Runner* critically comments on the photographic medium, see Marder (2012).

References

Alessio, D. (2005) "Redemption, 'race,' religion, reality and the far-right: Science fiction film adaptations of Philip K. Dick," in Brooker 2005a, 59–76.

Barad, J. (2007) "*Blade Runner* and Sartre: The boundaries of humanity," in M. Conard, ed., *The Philosophy of Neo-Noir*, Lexington KY: University Press of Kentucky, 21–34.

Barlow, A. (1997) "Philip K. Dick's androids: Victimized victimizers," in Kerman 1997, 76–89.

—— (2005) "Reel Toads and Imaginary Cities: Philip K. Dick, *Blade Runner* and the Contemporary Science Fiction Movie," in Brooker 2005a, 43–58.

Barr, M. (1997) "Metahuman 'kipple' or, do male movie makers dream of electric women?: Speciesism and sexism in *Blade Runner*," in Kerman 1997, 25–31.

Brooker, W., ed. (2005a) *The Blade Runner experience: The legacy of a science fiction classic*, New York: Columbia University Press.

—— (2005b) "Introduction: 2019 Vision," in Brooker 2005a, 1–10.

—— (2005c) "The Blade runner experience: pilgrimage and liminal space," in Brooker 2005a, 11–30.

Bukatman, S. (1997) *Blade Runner*, BFI modern classics, London: BFI.

—— (2012) *Blade Runner*, 2nd edn, BFI Film Classics, Houndmills: Palgrave Macmillan.

Carroll, N. (2006) "Introduction to the section on 'Art and Cognition,'" in N. Carroll and J. Choi, eds, *Philosophy of Film and Motion Pictures: An Anthology*, Oxford: Blackwell, 381–8.

Corliss, R. (2012) "*Blade Runner* at 30: Celebrating Ridley Scott's Dystopian Vision," *Time Magazine*, June 25, 2012.

Desser, D. (1997) "Race, space and class: The politics of the SF film from *Metropolis* to *Blade Runner*," in Kerman 1997, 110–23.

Ebert, R. (2010) *The Great Movies III*, Chicago: University of Chicago Press.

Fischer, R. (2007) "Interview: Charles de Laurizika," *chud.com*, August 2, available online at www.chud.com/11285/interview-charles-de-lauzirika-blade-runner (accessed June 14, 2014).

Ford, H. (2007) "Surviving Deckard: Harrison Ford on the toughest role of his career," *Empire (Blade Runner Special)*, December 2007, 78–80.

Galagher, N. (2002) "Bleak visions: Ridley Scott's *Blade Runner*: Director's cut," *Australian Screen Education Online*, 29: 169–73.

Gibson, W. (2003) *Pattern Recognition*, New York: Putnam.

—— (2011) Interview in the *Paris Review*, summer 2011, no. 197, available online at http://store.theparisreview.org/products/the-paris-review-no-197-summer-2011.

Gray, C. (2005) "Originals and Copies: The Fans of Philip K. Dick, Blade Runner and K.W. Jeter," in Brooker 2005a, 142–56.

Hills, M. (2005) "Academic Textual Poachers: Blade Runner as Cult Canonical Movie," in Brooker 2005a, 124–41.

—— (2011) *Blade Runner: Cultographies*, New York and London: Wallflower.

Howell, J. (2007) "What's New in Blade Runner: Final Cut?," *Sciencefictionworld.com*, December 9, available online at http://sciencefictionworld.com/films/science-fiction-films/156-whats-new-in-blade-runner-the-final-cut.html (accessed September 14, 2013).

Jermyn, D. (2005) "The Rachel Papers: In search of *Blade Runner*'s femme fatale," in Brooker 2005a, 159–72.

Kael, P. (1984) "Baby the Rain Must Fall," in P. Kael, *Taking it All In*, New York: Holt, Rinehart, and Winston, 360–5; first printed in *The New Yorker*, July 12, 1982.

Kellner, D., F. Liebowitz, and M. Ryan (1984) "*Blade Runner*: A diagnostic critique," *Jump Cut: A Review of Contemporary Media*, February 1984, 29: 6–8.

Kerman, J. (1997) *Retrofitting Blade Runner: Issues in Ridley Scott's Blade Runner and Philip K. Dick's Do Androids Dream of Electric Sheep?*, 2nd edn, Bowling Green OH: Bowling Green State University Popular Press.

—— (2005) "Post-Millenium Blade Runner," in Brooker 2005a, 1–10.

Knight, D., and G. McKnight (2008) "What is it to be human?: *Blade Runner* and *Dark City*," in S. Sanders, ed., *The Philosophy of Science Fiction Film*, Lexington: University Press of Kentucky, 21–37.

Kolb, W. M. (1990) "*Blade Runner*: An annotated bibliography," *Literature/Film Quarterly*, 18: 19–64.

—— (1997) "Script to screen: Blade runner in perspective," in Kerman 1997, 132–53.

Lucas, T. (1993) "Laser Discs: Blade Runner: Director's Cut," *Video Watchdog*, November/December, 20: 60–1.

Marder, E. (2012) "*Blade Runner*'s moving still," in *Mother in the Age of Mechanical Reproduction: Psychoanalysis, Photography, Deconstruction*, New York: Fordham University Press, 130–48.

Maslin, J. (1982) "Futuristic 'Blade Runner,'" *New York Times*, June 25, 1982.

Milner, A. (2004) "Darker Cities: Urban Dystopia and Science Fiction Cinema," *International Journal of Cultural Studies*, 7(3): 259–79.

Mulhall, S. (2002) *On Film*, London: Routledge.

—— (2007) "Picturing the human (body and soul): a reading of *Blade Runner*," *Film and Philosophy*, 1: 87–104.

—— (2008) *On Film*, 2nd edn, London: Routledge.

Nathan, I. (2007) "So Is He or Isn't He?," *Empire*, December 2007, 65.

Norris, A. (2013) "'How Can It Not Know What It Is?' Self and Other in Ridley Scott's Blade Runner," *Film-Philosophy*, 17(1): 19–50.

Redmond, S. (2005) "Purge! Class Pathology in *Blade Runner*," in Brooker 2005a, 173–89.

Sammon, P. (1993) "Do androids dream of unicorns? The Seven Faces of Blade Runner," *Video Watchdog*, 20: 32–59.

—— (1996) *Future noir: The Making of "Blade Runner"*, London: Orion Media.

—— (2007a) *Future noir: The Making of "Blade Runner"*, 2nd edn, London: Gollancz.

—— (2007b) "The Final Cut: The producer of the DVD fans have been waiting for talks," *Empire (Blade Runner Special)*, December 2007: 70–2.

Scott, R. (2007) "Interview with Paul M. Sammon," included as Appendix A in Sammon 2007a.

—— (2013) Interview with Ridley Scott available as an *Empire* podcast, October 28, 2013.

Sobchack, V. (1997) *Screening Space: the American Science Fiction Film*, 2nd edn, enlarged, New Brunswick, NJ: Rutgers University Press.

Turan, K. (1992) "Blade Runner 2," *Los Angeles Times Magazine*, September 13, 1992, 18–24.

Vejvoda, J. (2012) "Chris Nolan's Dark Knight Rises Movie Influences," *IGN.com*, July 30, available online at www.ign.com/articles/2012/07/30/chris-nolans-dark-knight-rises-movie-influences (accessed March 18, 2014).

Wartenberg, T. (2007) *Thinking on Screen: Film as Philosophy*, London and New York: Routledge.

Wood, R. (2003) *Hollywood from Vietnam to Reagan and Beyond*, expanded and revised, New York: Columbia University Press.

Yu, T. (2008) "Oriental Cities, Postmodern Futures: *Naked Lunch*, *Blade Runner* and *Neuromancer*," *Melus*, 33: 45–73.

Chapter 2

Berys Gaut

ELEGY IN LA

BLADE RUNNER, EMPATHY AND DEATH

BLADE RUNNER IS A FILM about robots (replicants), who are almost indistinguishable from humans, and about those who hunt them down and kill them (blade runners). At one point, Roy Batty, the leader of the replicants, manages by subterfuge to meet Eldon Tyrell, his human maker. A nervously stammering Tyrell asks of his creature, "What . . . ? What seems to be the problem?" Batty tersely replies, "Death".

Death is indeed the problem in *Blade Runner*. The film explores a trio of themes – death, empathy, and what it is to be human – and in so doing advances some cognitively rich and interesting views about their interconnections. And the way in which it does this plays a pivotal role in establishing the aesthetic and emotional power of this extraordinary film. The film is ultimately, I will argue, an elegy for humankind.

Death in *Blade Runner*

Blade Runner is a dark, death-obsessed film. The replicants have been built to live only four years, and for Batty the problem of death is pressing, since he is near the end of his allotted time. He and five other replicants have returned illegally to Earth to meet their maker and to get more life. But Tyrell tells Batty that he can do nothing – death is "a little out of my jurisdiction" – and Batty murders his less than omnipotent creator.

Figure 2.1 Still from *Blade Runner* (Final Cut) Dir. Ridley Scott (2007)

All six fugitive replicants are dead by the end of the film, five of them violently, whilst Batty dies when his lifespan expires.

Death in the film is ubiquitous: set in the decaying megalopolis of Los Angeles in 2019, it is about a world in which pollution has wiped out almost all animal life on Earth, which has largely been replaced by robotic replicas. The lighting, production design and music reflect the theme. The film is literally as well as metaphorically dark: lighting levels are low, punctuated by strafing beams from neon advertisements, and almost all scenes occur at night. Rain cascades down incessantly. Much of the city is decaying: the iconic Bradbury Building, in which the film's climax occurs, is leaking badly, filthy, cluttered with junk, and deserted apart from J. F. Sebastian, its sole human inhabitant. The Tyrell headquarters comprises two pyramids, evocative of death – for pyramids housed the royal dead and, in the Mayan version on which the headquarters are modelled, were sites of mass human sacrifice. The apartment of Rick Deckard, the blade runner of the title, also incorporates Mayan motifs, via the intermediary influence of the exterior of Frank Lloyd Wright's Ennis-Brown house (Sammon 2007: 136–7). The apartment is dark and tomb-like, its interior walls bare stone. And the music is a major contributor to the sombre mood: Vangelis's score for the film is lyrical, haunting and exquisitely sad, often based on a solitary saxophone lamenting over a synthesised wash of strings.

The film also links the short lifespan of the replicants to the mortality of humans through story devices. Sebastian suffers from Methuselah syndrome, which prematurely ages him, and so he stands as an intermediary between the replicants' restricted lifespan and the normal human one. He, like the other characters, is helpless before death: a genetic designer, he can do nothing to stop his own premature ageing, which confines him to the decaying Earth. And Gaff, Deckard's fellow blade runner, remarks of Rachael, the replicant with whom Deckard falls in love, "It's too bad she won't live. But then again, who does?" That pivotal line, occurring after Batty's death and Deckard's disavowal of his trade of killing, is repeated in Deckard's memory as the last line of the Final Cut version of the film (2007), which I am taking as my main target for interpretation.[1] The line serves several functions, not the least of which is to advert to the fact that the replicants' problem of a radically abbreviated life is merely a more extreme version of our own problem. The link is established even more firmly when the closing scene reveals that Deckard is himself a replicant; our main point of identification in the film, he has the limited four-year lifespan of the replicants.[2] The thought that the replicants' problem is merely a more extreme version of our own situation was particularly salient for Ridley Scott at the time that he agreed to direct *Blade Runner*, as his elder brother, to whom he had been very close, had recently died; his brother's death was indeed part of the reason that Scott agreed to take on the film, as he wanted to return rapidly to work.[3] Perhaps it is because of its resonance with a personal tragedy that he remarked that *Blade Runner* is "my most complete and personal film" (Sammon 2007: 444).

Empathy and being human

Though the centrality of death to the thematic structure of the film has been surprisingly little remarked on, the role of empathy and its importance to what it is to be human has been widely discussed.[4] Before returning to the role of death in *Blade Runner* we need first to examine this other theme.

Empathy is pivotal to the narrative, since the blade runners use the Voight-Kampff test, an empathy test, to determine who is a replicant. The device measures involuntary iris dilation, fluctuation of the pupil, and capillary dilation in response to a series of questions designed to evoke emotional and specifically empathetic reactions. The replicants give themselves away by displaying deficient empathetic responses. So the test establishes who is human by their capacity to feel empathy.

Deckard's problem is that he is starting to develop empathy. At the beginning of the film, he has retired from blade running, evidently having started to question what he is required to do, but is hauled back under duress by Bryant, the head of the blade runner unit, to "retire" the escaped replicants. Having killed the first of them, Zhora, he is left ashen and shaking. As he gradually falls in love with Rachael, his empathy for the replicants grows: and at the end of the film he tells Gaff that he is "finished". The film is in part about Deckard, as we naturally want to say, rediscovering his humanity.

Therein lies a difficulty. The film proposes the linkage of empathy to what it is to be human, shows its central character rediscovering his empathy and so his humanity, and then reveals that this character is a replicant and hence not human. The film seems incoherent. This is the strongest reason why many have sought to deny that Deckard is a replicant or to make it at least ambiguous whether he is. Scott Bukatman, in his book in the British Film Institute *Modern Classics* series, argues, "If Deckard *is* a replicant, then what's the moral of this story? The issue of human definition is clearly – to me – central to the work, and thus the *ambiguity* is crucial" (Bukatman 1997: 82). And the film director Frank Darabont argues that the movie doesn't work if Deckard is a replicant, since it is about Deckard "rediscovering his humanity".[5]

However, in the Final Cut version of the film (as well as the 1992 Director's Cut) the evidence for Deckard's replicant status is overwhelming. Crucially, these versions contain a short sequence where Deckard imagines or dreams a unicorn; at the end, Gaff leaves a tinfoil figure of a unicorn outside Deckard's apartment, signalling not only that he has been there and has spared Rachael, but also that he knows Deckard's innermost thoughts. The only plausible way in which he could have done so was if those thoughts were implants, and therefore if Deckard is a replicant.[6] The scene also echoes an earlier one in which Deckard convinces Rachael that she is a replicant by telling her about her memories, about which she has informed no one else, and explains that they are implants, which he has read about in her file. There are several pieces of ancillary evidence. Replicants' and robotic animals' eyes glow a characteristic red, and in the scene in his apartment, after Rachael has saved Deckard from another replicant, Leon, Deckard's eyes glow that characteristic red, slightly out of focus in the background. Deckard, like Leon and Rachael, is also obsessed by photographs. There are more subtle hints: Bryant gazes at Deckard in an oddly concerned and quizzical fashion after he tells him that replicants have only a four-year lifespan; and Gaff tells Deckard after Batty dies, "You've done a man's job, sir" – an odd remark, since Deckard does not kill Batty. In an alternate version of the scene, shot but not included in the film, Gaff goes on to say, "But are you sure you are a man? It's hard to tell who's who around here."[7] In the original 1982 release, the unicorn scene, though it had been filmed, was not included, and given the lesser evidentiary weight of the other clues, it's fair to say that it is indeterminate whether Deckard is a replicant in that cut. But the inclusion of the unicorn scene in the Director's and Final Cuts is decisive about Deckard's replicant status. Scott even remarked, albeit hyperbolically, in an interview, "Can't be any clearer than that. You don't get it, you're a moron."[8]

So we have a problem: the film is about how empathy makes us human, but its central character develops empathy only to discover that he is not human. But it is a mistake to conclude that the film is incoherent. "Human" has a biological and an evaluative sense. Biologically, the replicants are not strictly speaking human: they are made, not born; and they are genetically engineered, not naturally evolved. They are at most synthetic humans, not natural ones.[9] So in the biological sense, Deckard cannot rediscover his humanity. But there is also a well-entrenched evaluative use of that term, in which to exhibit one's humanity, to be human (or its cognate humane), is to be disposed to kindness, forgiveness and in general to be empathetic. In that sense Deckard discovers (though doesn't *re*discover) his humanity. The film proposes, then, that empathy is not confined to biological humans, but that replicants can possess it too. In fact, the argument that Deckard is not a replicant would not save the film from incoherence, if the biological sense of "humanity" were alone acknowledged, for Batty is never represented as anything other than a replicant, yet Batty, as we'll see, ends up exhibiting empathy.[10] To think that the replicants cannot show empathy, because they are not biological humans, and to discriminate against them because of their artificial status are instances of what Peter Singer (1986) calls *speciesism*. In opposing those speciesist tendencies, the film, far from being incoherent, makes an interesting point.[11] It is one that seems to have escaped even some of its makers: Harrison Ford, who plays Deckard, consistently argued during filming against suggesting that Deckard is a replicant, on the grounds that the audience needed an "emotional representative onscreen" – which begs the question of why such an identificatory figure must be a biological human.[12]

The Voight-Kampff test assumes that replicants cannot feel empathy – i.e. that only biological humans can feel empathy – and we have seen that the film's story contradicts this. The test also assumes that all biological humans feel empathy, for it needs to rule out false positives (i.e. identifying a human as a replicant). But the film also contradicts that claim, for the humans strikingly often lack empathy. Any replicant found on Earth is summarily executed: fail an empathy test and you are killed – thus demonstrating a spectacular lack of empathy in your human executioner. The blade runners are overtly deficient in empathy: Bryant calls the replicants "skin-jobs", echoing racist language (an implication brought out explicitly in the voice-over narration of the 1982 version); the killing of replicants is euphemistically named "retirement", not murder; a replicant is sometimes referred to as "it" rather than "he" or "she"; and the blade runners' murderous task requires them to be devoid of empathy for their victims. Rachael at one point asks Deckard, accusingly, "You know that Voight-Kampff test of yours, did you ever take that test yourself?" The replicants' makers also exhibit pronounced emotional detachment: Tyrell is acted by Joe Turkel in a cold, almost robotic manner, and wears formal attire and large trifocal glasses that seem to isolate him from his surroundings. The Tyrell Corporation's slogan for its replicants is "more human than human", but it sells them as slaves in off-world colonies, for use in hazardous situations, as soldiers and as "pleasure models". It has also designed them with a four-year lifespan to stop them, according to Bryant, developing "their own emotional responses". And it has implanted in at least some of them, including Rachael, Tyrell tells Deckard, false memories – supported by fake photographs – as a way to emotionally control them. So the replicants' particularly pressing problem of death, and the lack of empathy by which they are identified, have been deliberately designed into them. Tyrell observes Deckard's Voight-Kampff test of Rachael with amused superiority: he has misled him about Rachael being human, but by the end of the film we learn that his cynicism runs far deeper, for he is watching one of his replicants test another one. Nor is this lack of empathy confined to the blade runners and the Tyrell Corporation: anyone using a replicant for slave labour, military combat or sexual pleasure is employing a person barely distinguishable from a human in a degrading and demeaning fashion. So lack of empathy is endemic in biological humans; empathy is connected only to the evaluative notion of humanity.

Empathy and death

Interesting as it is, the film's sundering of empathy from biological humanity is not, I suggest, the most important thing that it has to say about empathy. For if empathy is not confined to biological humans, or even possessed by many of them, the question arises as to what sort of beings feel empathy. To answer that, we must return to the theme of death.

Blade Runner proposes an intimate relationship between empathy and awareness of mortality. Most of the questions that we hear posed in the Voight-Kampff test, designed to provoke empathy, concern animals' deaths: past, actual or threatened. For instance, someone gives you a calfskin wallet; a boy shows you his butterfly collection plus the killing jar; a tortoise lays on its back, its belly baking in the hot sun, beating its legs. Empathy is most powerfully evoked in relation to death. And, as we noted, Deckard's path to empathetic awakening begins with his growing revulsion at the murders he is required to commit.

The film's most sustained and interesting exploration of the connection between empathy and death centres on Roy Batty. Batty is a killer. First introduced in a video showing him during manufacture, Batty, explains Bryant, is a "combat model", designed for "optimum self-sufficiency". We see him next with Leon, tauntingly and menacingly questioning Chew, an old and helpless Chinese genetic engineer, about Tyrell; Chew is then, we can infer, murdered. The scene with which we began, Batty's confrontation with Tyrell, includes the most brutal murder of the film: Batty, having gently kissed Tyrell on the lips, then in close-up crushes his skull and gouges out his eyes. The gentle Sebastian, who has led Batty to Tyrell, is murdered offscreen. And in the film's climax, Batty engages in a deadly game of hide-and-seek, both terrifying and funny, with Deckard, who has just murdered Pris, Batty's replicant lover. Batty breaks the ring and little fingers of Deckard's gun hand, returns the gun to him, and gives him a head start as he hunts him up onto the roof of the Bradbury Building. Desperately jumping across to an adjacent building, Deckard misses, and is left dangling by his one good hand from a girder projecting over a vertiginous drop to the streets below. As he loses his grip and starts to fall, Batty grabs him by the arm and hauls him up. Batty, dying, then delivers the most moving speech of the film, a lament, an elegy for his brief life, to a dazed and crushed Deckard, a speech that begins, "I've seen things you people wouldn't believe."[13] Having shown every sign of intending to murder Deckard, Batty has rescued him and confided to him his deepest feelings.

Batty's transformation is underpinned by the religious iconography that attaches to him more richly than to any other character in the film. His first words are what sound like a quotation from Milton, but which are in fact rewritten lines from William Blake: "Fiery the angels fell, / Deep thunder rolled around their shores, / Burning with the fires of Orc."[14] Batty thus introduces himself as a fallen angel, a devil, and that allusion is visually echoed later as, having murdered Tyrell and Sebastian, he descends in an elevator, staring up at the stars as he plummets away from them. In his confrontation with Tyrell, religious imagery multiplies. "It's not an easy thing to meet your maker", he tells Tyrell, and then asks him to solve the problem of death. Batty threateningly petitions, "I want more life, father". Tyrell, whose apartment is festooned with long candles that recall a church, and whose bed is modelled after that of Pope John Paul II (Kolb 1997: 166), describes Batty as the Prodigal Son. But this is no reformed prodigal, as Tyrell soon discovers. Yet during the climactic chase of Deckard, the iconography transforms. Feeling his life slip away, Batty is desperate to hold onto it a little longer, pulls out a nail from the floor and drives it through the palm of his hand, to gain focus through pain. After this self-crucifixion he cradles a white dove, the symbol of peace and the Holy Spirit, in his left hand. As he dies, the dove flutters away, Batty's soul departing. A replicant has become a person, a devil has become a saviour.

The film leaves it somewhat open as to why Batty saves Deckard. But the plausible explanations refer to empathy and Batty's appreciation that his own death is near.[15] As he watches Deckard dangle from the girder, Batty stares at him intensely, intermittently with impish glee, and says, "Quite an experience to live in fear, isn't it? That's what it is to be a slave." He has got Deckard to feel what Batty has felt all of his life; and he has done so because Deckard is in abject terror of death. As Batty gazes down at Deckard he twice narrows his eyes, focussing, as if seeing Deckard anew: he sees someone, like himself, who is about to die and

Figure 2.2 Still from *Blade Runner* (Final Cut) Dir. Ridley Scott (2007)

is in pain and feeling fear. Out of that common bond of feeling, Batty unexpectedly saves his persecutor. So death plays a central role in Batty's empathetic response to Deckard, both because of the intensity of the fear it provokes and because they both immediately face the prospect of their demise. And in recounting the marvellous sights he has seen, Batty shows us that by the end of his life he has a rich set of memories and that these give him a sense of being a continuing self, distinct from others. He can thereby appreciate that the loss through death of such individual, unique selves, whether of himself or Deckard, is all the more poignant and terrible.[16]

Death plays a further role in Batty's motivation: his moving final speech laments the loss of life, of what he has seen, of his experiences of unique and beautiful things. It is an expression of his love of life, and that love of life is so intense that he seems to want life's continuance, no matter who has it. This is made explicit in Deckard's voice-over narration in the 1982 version: "Maybe in those last moments he loved life more than he ever had before. Not just life. Anybody's life. My life." And although Batty's death means that no one will directly recall the wonderful sights he has witnessed, in saving Deckard he leaves someone to whom he can convey them, and so pass on and share his sense of wonder at what he has seen, thus rescuing something from his own destruction.

These reflections suggest that what Batty feels for Deckard at the end is empathy, and the reason that he does so is that they both face death. Empathy is a matter of sharing an emotion, of feeling what another is feeling, because one projects oneself imaginatively into his or her position (Gaut 2010a: ch. 6; and Gaut 2010b). Few feelings are as intense as fear of death, and one's imagining of another's situation is greatly aided by being in, or believing that one shortly will be in, that situation oneself. So death, both as a universal feature of life and as the provoker of extreme emotions, is well suited to be the cause and the object of empathetic emotion. Moreover, in confronting death, and thus in being deprived of all future possibility of sharing, there is an urgent psychological need to share emotionally one last time, to empathise with another creature, to pass on something of one's emotional life to someone else, however temporarily and imperfectly. Empathy and mortality are linked, then, for the fear of death and ultimate loss is a key cause of empathetic emotions in creatures who can feel such things. And in an affective confirmation of this link it is at the moment of his death that we, the audience, finally and unambiguously feel empathy for Batty, that part-devil, part-saviour.

These points fit well with our earlier observations that the Voight-Kampff questions are primarily about death and that Deckard begins his journey to empathy through revulsion at killing. And his other route to empathy, through his love of Rachael, is also affected by his experience of death and suffering. When he first discovers that Rachael is a replicant, he asks Tyrell, "How can it not know what it is?" And when Rachael comes to his apartment to try to persuade him and reassure herself that she is not a replicant, he is brutal in stripping her of her illusions. Only when she starts to weep does he soften. After he kills Zhora, and Rachael saves his life by killing Leon, he reaches out to her emotionally, sympathising with the "shakes" they both feel. He tries to console her, "It's part of the business." In a brilliantly written rebuttal, she replies, "I'm not in the business . . . I am the business." The scene culminates in Deckard's seduction of her in the corridor of his apartment. She tries to leave, he slams the door; and lit in a striating chiaroscuro of light through half-closed blinds, he instructs her to say what she has to say to acquiesce in his desires. Despite its erotic charge, the scene has a disturbing rape-like quality, and powerfully conveys that Deckard is still treating her as a thing. It is only after his final encounter with Batty, and so with his own experience of nearly dying and of having someone reach out to him in death, that he finally treats Rachael as a person. Unlike in their earlier enforced conversation, he asks her, "Do you love me?" and she freely answers, "I love you"; he asks her, "Do you trust me?" and she freely replies, "I trust you". Only after nearly dying, then, does he finally acknowledge that he is dealing with another person, for he has experienced for himself that tenuous mortality that he already knew to be hers too.

Film, philosophy and elegy

I have argued, then, that the film proposes a connection of empathy not with biological humanity, but with an evaluative notion of humanity that is applicable to other beings too; and that it also suggests, through its multifarious linking of death with empathy, that death is powerfully suited to evoke empathetic responses, because of the universal nature of that condition, the strong emotions it evokes, and the need to share emotionally before that last moment when sharing is no longer possible. Death and its concomitant empathetic emotions also condition and inflect emotions such as romantic love, showing the lover and beloved to be on a par as mortals, bound to a common fate.

Some will take these claims as supporting the doctrine that films can do philosophy, and *Blade Runner* has been proposed as such a film (Wartenberg 2007: 1–3). It is true that films can do some of what philosophy does: they can suggest claims, illustrate them, get us to think about and imagine situations in which they are in play, test them against our affective reactions and detailed imaginative investigation, and so on. But they are also unlike philosophy, in that they rarely make their general claims explicit, or advance general arguments for them, or propose carefully crafted and precise distinctions; and were they to do so, this would be apt to wreck their aesthetic value. To say that films can do some of the things that philosophy does is not to say that they *are* forms of philosophy. We should agree that they can function cognitively and that this is under certain conditions part of their aesthetic value, but this is not to say that they do philosophy, for not all forms of cognition are philosophical ones.[17] And films typically have aims, such as moving us emotionally and aesthetically, that philosophy rarely embraces.

The aesthetic power of *Blade Runner* is achieved in part through the bleak plausibility of its cognitive vision and through the way that, as we have seen, that vision is expressed or suggested through the artistic elements of the film – its plot, characterisation, acting, production design and music. Even the nature of the beauty of the film plays a role in expressing its vision. *Blade Runner* is one of the most visually dense and strikingly beautiful films ever created, yet it finds its beauty in transience, decomposition and death: in fireballs erupting from petrochemical cracking towers; in neon displays shrilly contesting with the surrounding gloom; in laser-like beams from advertising blimps strafing the night; in decaying apartments; in garbage piled outside buildings; in the visual cacophony of crushingly crowded streets; in the fleeting movements of smoke, of rain, of shadow and light; in the death of Zhora, as she crashes through panes of shattering glass; in Batty's final, eloquent, quiet demise. This is the beauty of evanescence, decay and death, evocative of the larger vision of the film. It recalls what Rainer Maria Rilke (1939: 25) wrote in another elegy, "For Beauty's nothing / but beginning of Terror we're still just able to bear, / and why we adore it so is because it serenely / disdains to destroy us."

In coupling together empathy and death, the film also suggests that empathy finds its natural and most powerful artistic voice in elegy, in the lament for the loss of life. The whole film is an elegy, in its sad and beautiful dwelling on the theme of death, and Batty elegises for himself at the end of the film. But in elegising for himself, he also elegises for us. The replicants are, considered as an artistic and cognitive device, ourselves driven to a limit: more powerful, intelligent and living more intensely than we do, but also more radically curtailed in their lifespan than are we. They represent ourselves, both our strengths and our mortal weakness, taken to an extreme. In asking us to consider this extreme case, the film invites reflection on our own mortality, and therein resides much of its power. Its closing line, recall, is "It's too bad she won't live. But then again, who does?" And its final image is the elevator door closing on Rachael, who has no more than four years to live, and on Deckard, who must be nearing the end of his four-year span; for no one would design a killer with crippling doubts who has developed his "own emotional responses", which a four-year lifespan was designed to curtail.

So at the end of the film the elevator door closes on Rachael and Deckard, a kind of visual entombment of two creatures in love who will shortly die, one of whom has been our main identificatory point throughout the film, and with the line echoing in our thoughts that their situation is ours, delineated more sharply by the radical paring down of their lives. *Blade Runner* is thus a lament for the dead, a lament for the dying, a lament for the soon-to-be dead. It is, in short, a lament for us.[18]

Notes

1 Sammon (2007: 570) calculates that there are seven versions of the film. The two most important for my purposes are the Final Cut version, 2007, which is Scott's final and preferred version, and the original 1982 theatrical release in its international version. The Director's Cut, 1992, like the Final Cut, differs from the original release most importantly in lacking its happy ending and its voice-over narration, and in including the unicorn scene.

2 Deckard's replicant status is still, surprisingly, controversial: I will return to the point and the significance of the resistance to it in the next section.

3 See Sammon (2007: 48) and also the first section of *Dangerous Days: Making Blade Runner* on DVD 2 of the five-disc Complete Collector's Edition of *Blade Runner*, Warner Bros and the Blade Runner Partnership, 2007.

4 For instance, the index to Kerman (1997), a collection of academic essays on the film and Dick's source novel, lists 15 entries under "empathy", 15 under "humanity", but only one under "death" – and this is a reference to a short story by Larry Niven.

5 Interview in "Deck-a-Rep: The True Nature of Rick Deckard" (DVD 4 of the Complete Collector's Edition).

6 Bukatman (1997: 82) suggests that the unicorn could be an archetype representing Rachael; but even if that were so, how does Gaff know that Deckard has thought of her that way?

7 See "Deleted and Alternate Scenes" (DVD 4 of the Complete Collector's Edition).

8 Interview in "Deck-a-Rep".

9 The original opening sequence, included on the Workprint (DVD 5 of the Complete Collector's Edition), which was used for test screenings, was a quotation from the fictional New American Dictionary, 2016, which defines "replicant" as a "synthetic human". None of the other versions of the film use this opening.

10 This is a striking difference to the source novel (Dick 2004), where the replicants are shown as entirely lacking in empathy, and this difference plays an important role in explaining the greater richness of the film compared to the book.

11 Barr (1997) also notes the speciesism theme.

12 See Sammon (2007: 56) and also Ford's interview in "Deck-a-Rep".

13 The speech was originally drafted by one of the scriptwriters, David Peoples; Rutger Hauer, who plays Batty, shortened it radically and improvised its great closing lines: "All those moments will be lost in time like tears in rain. Time to die." Hauer also came up with the idea of holding and releasing the dove (Sammon 2007: 192–6). As this illustrates, multiple authorship has considerable artistic importance in this film (see also Gaut 2010a: 129).

14 See Desser (1997: 64), who also brings out the religious imagery in the film well. Significantly, in Blake's poem the angels rose, not fell.

15 At one point Scott told Hauer that he did not know why Batty saves Deckard, other than simply because of a reflex action of grabbing (Sammon 2007: 194). If this action were a mere reflex and if Batty had wanted to kill Deckard, he would have let go immediately after having it.

16 Thanks to David Davies for the observation about the role of memory here. It is not clear whether any replicants other than Rachael (who Tyrell tells Deckard is an "experiment") and Deckard have implanted memories, but Batty has had almost four years to accumulate real ones.

17 For a defence of aesthetic cognitivism, see Gaut (2007: ch. 7 and ch. 8).

18 I would like to thank Robert Burgoyne, Amy Coplan, David Davies and George Wilson, as well as participants in the *Film, Philosophy and Death* conference, University of York, 2011, for their helpful comments on this paper.

References

Barr, M. (1997) "Metahuman 'Kipple' Or, Do Male Movie Makers Dream of Electric Women?: Speciesism and Sexism in *Blade Runner*" in Kerman (ed.) 1997, 25–31.

Bukatman, S. (1997) *Blade Runner*, London: British Film Institute.

Desser, D. (1997) "The New Eve: The Influence of *Paradise Lost* and *Frankenstein* on *Blade Runner*" in Kerman (ed.) 1997, 53–65.

Dick, P. K. (2004) *Do Androids Dream of Electric Sheep?* in his *Five Great Novels*, London: Gollancz.

Gaut, B. (2007) *Art, Emotion and Ethics*, Oxford: Oxford University Press.

—— (2010a) *A Philosophy of Cinematic Art*, Cambridge: Cambridge University Press.

—— (2010b) "Empathy and Identification in Cinema", *Midwest Studies in Philosophy*, XXXIV: 136–57.

Kerman, J. B. (ed.) (1997) *Retrofitting Blade Runner: Issues in Ridley Scott's Blade Runner and Philip K. Dick's Do Androids Dream of Electric Sheep?*, 2nd edn, Madison: University of Wisconsin Press.

Kolb, W. M. (1997) "*Blade Runner* Film Notes" in Kerman (ed.) 1997, 154–77.

Rilke, R. M. (1939) *Duino Elegies*, trans. J. B. Leishman and Stephen Spender, London: Hogarth Press.

Sammon, P. M. (2007) *Future Noir: The Making Of Blade Runner*, 2nd edn, London: Orion.

Singer, P. (1986) "All Animals are Equal" in P. Singer (ed.), *Applied Ethics*, Oxford: Oxford University Press, 215–28.

Wartenberg, T. E. (2007) *Thinking on Screen: Film as Philosophy*, London: Routledge.

Further reading

Amy Coplan and Peter Goldie (eds) (2012) *Empathy: Philosophical and Psychological Perspectives*, Oxford: Oxford University Press. (A comprehensive collection of papers on empathy by philosophers and psychologists.)

Murray Smith and Thomas E. Wartenberg (eds) (2006) *Thinking through Cinema: Film as Philosophy*, Malden, MA: Blackwell. (Papers by philosophers and film theorists discussing whether films can do philosophy, both in general and in respect of particular films.)

Chapter 3

Peter Atterton

"MORE HUMAN THAN HUMAN"

BLADE RUNNER AND BEING-TOWARD-DEATH

We were born to die.
(*Romeo and Juliet*, 3.4.4)

Introduction

Tyrell: Commerce is our goal here at Tyrell. More human than human is our motto.

ONE OF THE MOST lamentable aspects of discussions about Ridley Scott's film *Blade Runner*[1] is the way in which they rapidly turn into a discussion of whether Deckard is a replicant, when the really interesting philosophical question is what makes the replicants *human*. We want to know just how a robot that by definition is a machine is able to express whatever is characteristic of human beings. The answer to this question would matter less if the film did not also challenge our preconceptions about what it means to be human. What are we to make of the claim of the powerful biotech engineering firm Tyrell Corporation that replicants are "more human than human"? How do they surpass the humanity of the biological humans who create and "retire" them? ("Retirement" is the euphemism used by special police units – "Blade Runner squads" – to refer to the hunting down and killing of trespassing replicants.) Shall we simply say (quoting the film's crawl), "Replicants

Figure 3.1 Still from *Blade Runner* (Theatrical Cut) Dir. Ridley Scott (1982)

were superior in strength and agility, and at least equal in intelligence, to the genetic engineers who created them"? No, since strength and agility are not characteristically *human* traits. Do replicants express their humanity insofar as they are superiorly intelligent? No, because people with inferior levels of intelligence are no less human for all that. What then is the status of the claim that replicants are "more human than human"?

A human being is obviously not merely a machine that acts in a rigid, mechanical, or unconscious manner, but is an animate, living (or, what is sometimes called "lived") body. According to Plato in the *Republic* (Book IV: 435c–441c), the "mind" or "soul" (*psyche*) that animates the human body embraces three different faculties or powers: intelligence, emotions, and bodily desires. Replicants are supposed to have intelligence and desires, but not emotions, though their designers suggested that in time they might develop their "own emotional responses." For many movie aficionados it is the replicants' possession of emotions and passions that ultimately serves to close the gap between them and us. This, indeed, has a ring of truth about it. However, I wish to suggest that while all these aspects of our nature are entitled to be called "human," none of them, not even the capacity for the emotional transference we call "empathy," which is shared by other primate species (see de Waal, 2009), indicates the essential hallmark of the human. I shall not defend that claim here, but turn instead to a characteristic that I think indicates the *humanus* of man in an unambiguous way. A person, unlike any other animal I am aware of, is a being that *knows he or she is going to die*. It is the dread of dying that is human *par excellence*. Heidegger (after Lucretius and

Montaigne) has made the case better than anybody: "The mortals are the human beings. They are called mortals because they can die. To die means to be capable of death *as* death. Only man dies, and indeed continually, as long as he remains on earth" (1971: 150). As we shall see below, it is precisely this capacity for death *as* death that is shared by the replicants in the film, all of whom have a built-in obsolescence, a four-year lifespan, with an abrupt "termination date." Replicants live on earth knowing they are going to die. In Heidegger's language, their lives are lived as "being-toward-death." Herein lies their humanity.

The futurity of death

The reason why death is so important in Heidegger is that only death can make us recognize the importance of life. It is only when we realize that we are mortal, and thus that our time on earth is limited, that we are reminded that life is precious, fragile, and short. Only death puts an unsurpassable limit on life and by recognizing that limit we are thrown back into life. Death is, as it were, the horizon of life – the infinite expanse of nothingness that gives us a perspective on life and its possibilities. *Blade Runner* is really, then, about how *truly valuable* life is in view of the fact that there is nothing else. This may not seem obvious given the film's noirish cynicism, gloomy setting (the Los Angeles 2019 megalopolis was nicknamed "Hades" by the film's crew [Sammon, 1996: 231]), and unsentimental portrayal of violence. How can life have value when it can be lived so emptily and self-destructively, and extinguished so easily? However, I think the way the replicants live and die in *Blade Runner* suggests quite the opposite. This is particularly apparent in the case of that paradigm Nexus-6 replicant Roy Batty, the replicant in the film whose life force (*vis vitalis*) is particularly strong.

In Roy, the hero of the film, we are presented with someone whose life is in every way exceptional and when he dies we sense that something truly extraordinary has been lost forever. His first words are revelatory of his nature. We see a close-up of his anemic right hand cramping up, and hear him saying, "Time enough." By this he means there is still time to find a way to postpone his death. I say "postpone," because it is never a question of Roy seeking some *lapis philosophorum*. Roy seeks "more life," not eternal life. The whole of his tragic being can be characterized by this obstinate refusal to accept his fate, the fact that he was *made* "not to last." Thus his cramping right hand comes to symbolize both his premature senescence and an attempt to "seize" a last chance to be against death. As Levinas says, "Prior to death there is always a last chance; this is what heroes seize, not death" (1987: 73). Roy, like all true heroes – like the Scottish warrior Macbeth who chooses to fight Macduff despite the fact that his fate is sealed and death is imminent ("Though Birnam Wood be come to Dunsinane, / And thou opposed, being of no woman born, / Yet I will try the last" [*Macbeth*, 5.8.30–32; quoted by Levinas, 1987: 73]) – seizes one last opportunity in life to be against death. But there is also something terribly Faustian about this "prodigal son." I am not just thinking of Marlowe's Faust, who must die at an appointed hour before he is ready, and so "cut is the branch that might have grown full straight" (*Doctor Faustus*, 5.3.16). I also have in mind Goethe's protagonist, who desperately seeks to rescue Helen from Hades and draw her into life. This extraordinary ambition spurs Manto the Prophetess to remark: "I love him who desires the impossible" (*Faust*, 2: 7488). Consider what Roy says to Pris in Sebastian's apartment after he brings her the news of the death of Leon, another replicant:

Roy: Ah [weeping]. . . . There's only two of us now.
Pris: Then we're stupid and we'll die.
Roy: [Smile] No we won't.

One can legitimately ask whether Roy's stubborn refusal to accept the inevitable is evidence of what Heidegger called "inauthentic Being-toward-death." In *Being and Time*, Heidegger observed that for the most part we seek to flee in the face of death by concealing its true nature as something that is both *certain* and *indefinite* in that it can happen at any moment. In treating death as something that is going to happen "but not right away" (Heidegger, 1962: 302), we evade thinking about not just our dying but ourselves as ones who must live knowing that they must eventually die. But it is easily seen that this "tranquilization about death" (298) cannot be countenanced in Roy's case. When Roy says to Pris, "No we won't" he is not denying the Heideggerian observation that death *will happen*. Indeed, it is because he is all too certain that it will happen sooner rather than later if he does not act that he says to

Sebastian: "If we don't find help soon, Pris hasn't got long to live. We can't allow that." But while this is no basis for saying that Roy is inauthentically deferring death to some time in the distant future, it does suggest that it is in the nature of death that it is always *to come*. Heidegger himself seems to acknowledge something like this when he describes death as a "not yet" (1962: 284), the same phrase that Roy uses when his hand cramps for a second time in the penultimate scene of the film, suggesting that *death* is always future. Why? Because the possibility of death is the one possibility that will never be actualized for the person who is dying. The moment it becomes real the person whose death it is is annihilated. The idea here is an old one and goes back to Epicurus, who wrote in his *Letter to Menoeceus*: "If you are, it is not; if it is, you are not." What this means is that "death is never a present" (Levinas, 1987: 71). Death and the one who is dying will never become contemporaries of each other, such that the moribund always has time, no matter how infinitesimally small, to be against the death that is perpetually future.

Creaturely superiority

The Roy we meet in the film has done "extraordinary things," a top-notch combat model who has escaped the off-world colonies, jumped a shuttle, traversed the Tannhäuser Gate, become the leader of a band of renegades, but who galls under the realization that all this is insignificant before his sense of limitation, of finitude, symbolized by his termination date. But it is precisely Roy's superior physical and mental attributes that sustain his drive for freedom, growth, and the overcoming of barriers. He can be tender and loving (witness his kiss on the lips of the corpse of his beloved Pris as he puts her protruding tongue back into her mouth), and then violent and ruthless (crushing Tyrell's skull). His searing eloquence (deliberately misquoting Blake[2]) gives way on occasion to goofball behavior (making a comic face with buckteeth and holding up two glass eyes over his own as he says to J. F. Sebastian: "We're so happy you found us"). He is the most childish of men ("Ah, gosh. You've really got some nice toys here") and the most grave ("Time to die"). He is a soldier and a philosopher, a man of action and a man of reflection. Does he care about the lives of his fellow replicants? Or is he only out to save himself and his girlfriend? Is he admirable or detestable? He loves life but is prepared to kill to extend his own. On at least one occasion, as we will see, he is stricken with guilt; but most of the time he appears to have no conscience at all. His life remains a refusal until the very last moments, when he appears to accept the inevitable. In sum he is, without wishing to sound glib, a man who resists easy categorization. To speak of Roy as *x* or *y*, hero or villain, is already to have misrepresented him. I called him a "hero" earlier but he is not what normally passes as a hero in the Philistine sense. Certainly he is not a Christ-figure as some commentators have suggested (Shapiro, 1993: 99). Roy – *Raj? Roi?* (King?)[3] – is not on earth to redeem mankind by dying for our sins; he is the redeemer who wants to live, who redeems humanity by showing human beings what their possibilities are, who in his struggle *against* death opens up new horizons *in life* that tell of freedom, strength, and self-overcoming. He is a hero in the same way that Satan is the hero of Milton's *Paradise Lost* and the Creature the hero of Shelley's *Frankenstein* (see Desser, 1991), i.e. someone whose life has accomplished great things but whose great wounds have caused a hemorrhage of the moral sense so much so that he is forever barred from the kingdom of heaven.

It is impossible not to be reminded here of Nietzsche. In *Thus Spoke Zarathustra* Nietzsche gives expression to the idea of two types of humanity: the Overmen (the future "Masters of the Earth"), those unique and exceptional individuals who give themselves the law, whose ethics is one of pure self-affirmation (such as we find in Roy), and their complete opposite, "the last man," who represents a declining humanity reduced to a servile herd animal in search of happiness. Nietzsche refers to this nihilistic and gregarious humanity as "little people" (*kleinen Leute*) (1978: 287), which coincidentally is the exact term used in *Blade Runner* to describe the underclass of humanity left on earth, made up of street-merchants, opium smokers, punks, etc., all speaking the same "gibberish" called "city-speak, guttertalk, a mismash of Japanese, Spanish, German, what have you." But the Overman also stands above what Nietzsche calls the "higher man," the individual who continues to uphold a secular ideal (science) in the wake of the collapse of all other values on earth, parodied in *Thus Spoke Zarathustra* by the scientist who scrupulously inspects part of "the leech" (248–51), which sucks the life out of him. In the film, the conscientious seeker of knowledge at all costs is represented by the brilliant scientist Hannibal Chew, who is satisfied using (up) what "little time" he has left on earth admiring small things: eyes.

The visual image of the half-frozen Chew working in a laboratory, wearing a thick, rigid fur coat is suggestive of *rigor mortis*. He is hunched over a workbench muttering to himself (in Chinese) as he examines a replicant eye under a microscope:

> Chew: Ha, yes! So little time.
> Ha, ha! So beautiful.
> Ha, ha! Beautiful indeed!
>
> (Sammon, 1996: 133)

In a film so intently focused on the sense of vision (e.g. the Voight-Kampff Test), the nuances of the eye, both seeing and seen, subject and object, will prove to be one of the most powerful complexes of images. Here the eye (really, "eyeball") is merely looked at; it is solely an object of scientific study and investigation. But it raises a question that has philosophical implications. The question is what Kierkegaard called the question of "life's definition" – i.e. the question of "whether it is justifiable to use one's whole life for this" (1967: 404). To be sure, I don't wish to suggest that the pursuit of scientific knowledge is meaningless, but I do think that *Blade Runner* presents a Romantic vision of the world that shows that it is not intellect but experience that counts; not pure knowledge, but life. For Roy there are more things in heaven and earth than are dreamed of in Chew's philosophy.

Roy reaches for scientific knowledge, but only as a means, never as an end in itself:

> Roy: Yes, questions. . . . Morphology. Longevity. Incept dates.

Chew's anxiousness standing before Roy is expressed in his rapid-fire response: "Don't know – I, I don't know such stuff. I just do eyes. Just eyes – just genetic design – just eyes. You Nexus, huh? I design your eyes." Roy's rejoinder is light and ironic rather than caustic and disparaging, a cleverly constructed amphiboly (a sentence ambiguous because of its construction) that points up Chew's poverty of vision: "Chew, if only you could see what I've seen with your eyes." Chew has only seen Roy's eyes – he has not seen what Roy has seen *with* them.

The counterfactual hints at the sense that he is not capable of seeing what Roy has seen, that he lacks the power to experience what Roy experiences.

The scene in which Roy first meets another one of his "makers" for the first time, J. F. Sebastian, is evidence of Roy's creaturely superiority once more. Roy asks Sebastian why he is "staring" at him and Pris. Sebastian replies: "Because. You're so different. You're so perfect." Sebastian proceeds to ask what generation of replicant they are, and when he is told they are Nexus 6, exultantly exclaims: "Ah, I knew it. 'Cause I do genetic design work for the Tyrell Corporation. There's some of me in you." Like Chew's "I designed your eyes," Sebastian's reply does more than merely claim credit for some aspect of the way Roy turned out. It suggests that Roy's existence is worthy of taking credit for, as though, in almost Whitmanesque fashion, in celebrating Roy he were celebrating himself. The reality, of course, is that Sebastian and Roy are as different as chalk and cheese. Scott presents Sebastian as an ingenuous and good-natured idiot savant who "stays put," i.e. someone who is incapable of the kind of self-overcoming and transcendence that we see in Roy. He is easily manipulated and does as he is told. When Roy tells him to "stay here" after he gains entry to Tyrell's suite, all he can do is passively watch as Roy crushes Tyrell's skull, before himself turning to run away. Sebastian illustrates what Nietzsche calls "the human-all-too-human" – those who, in Walter Kaufmann's words, "spend their lives fleeing themselves, their task, and their loneliness" (1974: 310).

I am trying to suggest by these examples that Roy, though he is "merely" an android, represents the humanity of man better than any human. It is not simply that he is a Cartesian *res cogitans* – "a thinking thing." Here is a striking example that is intended to appeal to philosophers. In the course of his first meeting with Roy, Sebastian requests that he perform tricks for him. "Show me something," says Sebastian. "Like what?" asks Roy. "Like anything," suggests Sebastian. At this point Roy indignantly replies, "We're not computers Sebastian, we're physical," whereupon Pris adds, "I think, Sebastian, therefore I am." Roy then says: "Very good Pris, now show him why." Pris obliges by performing an elegant back walkover, before quickly plunging her hand into a boiling pan of water to retrieve a boiled egg, which she then tosses at Sebastian, who catches it and then drops it because it is too hot. It is the relation to the *lived body* (not the *mind*) evinced by the remark "we're physical" (from the Greek *phusis*, meaning "nature") that defines the human in this scene. Roy is not merely a computer; he is physical in the sense of *being alive*. Only a being that is alive can die. But Roy does not die in the same way as other living beings, plants, or animals, for example. The human that merely "perishes" (*verendet*) like other organisms, according to Heidegger, does not authentically die at all. He does not self-consciously think about death as a possibility that is both inescapable and indefinite. (This is also very different from the type of inhuman/e death that Hemingway in *Death in the Afternoon* likens to death on the battlefield: "The first thing you found about the dead was that, hit badly enough, they died like animals. . . . I do not know, but most men die like animals, not men" [1960: 113].) Roy does not die like a (mere) animal; he dies like a man.

Sebastian too is dying – literally. The 25-year-old engineering genius suffers from premature aging called "Methuselah syndrome":

Roy: We've got a lot in common.
Sebastian: What do you mean?
Roy: Similar problems.
Pris: Accelerated decrepitude.

The difference between Roy and Sebastian is not their death – but the ways they live. Or, rather, it would be better to say that the difference lies in their respective ways in which they face their death during the time that they have left. Sebastian has but little time left on earth (implausibly, he is prohibited from going to the Off-World due to his condition), but lives as though he has an unlimited time ahead of him. He lives a lonely and alienated existence, which consists of routinely going to work each day and returning home each evening to his toys, which mechanically greet him at the door, as regular as clockwork ("Home again, home again, jiggity jig. Good evening J. F."). When Pris asks him if he is lonely, he replies: "Not really. I make friends. They're toys. My friends are toys. I make them. It's a hobby." The hobby comes to symbolize a preoccupation with which Sebastian is mindlessly infatuated in order to *kill time* at the same time as giving him the illusion of freedom and purpose. Sebastian shows no signs of living in what Heidegger in *Being and Time* called "essential anxiety" (1962: 310) in the face of death and having his routine and routinized life "shattered" (308) by its imminence.

We can't escape the conclusion that the passive and lonely Sebastian, who craves companionship to the point where he has to literally "make friends," is a perfect foil for the active and aggressive Roy whose solitude is one that cannot be assuaged by friends, lovers, or company, since it is a matter, as Heidegger said, of always dying alone. Speaking of *Dasein* (being-there) – Heidegger's term for *human* being – he writes:

> With death, Dasein stands before itself in its ownmost potentiality-for-being. This is a possibility in which the issue is nothing less than Dasein's being-in-the-world. Its death is the possibility of no-longer-being-able-to-be-there. If Dasein stands before itself as this possibility, it has been fully assigned to its ownmost potentiality-for-being. When it stands before itself in this way, all its relations to any other Dasein have been undone. This ownmost nonrelational possibility is at the same time the uttermost one.
>
> (1962: 294)

To say that in death "all its relations to any other Dasein have been undone" is not to say that *Dasein* is empirically alone when it dies, which is not true for everyone and certainly not true of Roy, as we will see. What Heidegger means is that dying is essentially something that each of us will have to do in our own way (hence Heidegger calls it one's "*ownmost*" possibility), without anybody else being able to do one's dying for one. As Luther put it in his "Eight Wittenberg Sermons of 1522": "The summons of death come to us all, and no one can die for another. Everyone must fight his own battle with death by himself, alone. We can shout into another's ears, but everyone must himself be prepared for the time of death, for I will not be with you then, nor you with me" (quoted by Bernasconi, 2000). In other words, nobody can be a representative for another when it comes to death. According to whether one tries in moments of lucidity to reconcile oneself with this fact (Roy) or whether one adopts the banal everyday selfhood that is no longer troubled by death (Sebastian) will determine whether or not death has the power to individualize one, and in so doing turn one into what Heidegger calls an "authentic self."

The facts of life

I have said almost nothing so far about the scene in the film that deals with the mock religious aspects of Roy's being-toward-death. The scene belongs to the rising action of the film but also contains climactic elements, for it is here that Roy has an epiphany that marks a change, for the worse, in his fortunes. Roy goes to meet "his maker," Dr. Eldon Tyrell, in the hope that he will be able to prolong his life. But when he finds him in his penthouse suite atop the giant Tyrell pyramid – a fitting thanatophobic symbol – he finds only a Wizard of Oz-type, hiding behind huge spectacles and a quilted dressing gown, who does not have the answers he is searching for:

Tyrell: What seems to be the problem?
Roy: Death.
Tyrell: Death. Well, I'm afraid that's a little out of my jurisdiction, you –
Roy: I want more life, fucker![4]
Tyrell: The facts of life.

Tyrell tells him that "to make an alteration in the evolvement of an organic life system is fatal." Roy desperately moots possible alternatives: "EMS recombination," "a repressor protein that blocks the operating cells." But to no avail. They've all been tried before – "Ethyl methane sulfonate as an alkylating agent and a potent mutagen." According to Tyrell, "it created a virus so lethal the subject was dead before we left the table." *The exchange quickly devolves into a conversation in which Tyrell's absolute incapacity to empathize with his creation is in full view:*

Tyrell: But, this – all of this is academic. You were made as well as we could make you.
Roy: But not to last.
Tyrell: The light that burns twice as bright burns half as long. And you have burned so very, very brightly, Roy. Look at you. You're the prodigal son. You're quite a prize!
Roy: I've done questionable things.
Tyrell: Also extraordinary things. Revel in your time!
Roy: Nothing the god of biomechanics wouldn't let you in heaven for. . . .

It seems to me that Tyrell stands to Roy's confession more as the impatient father to the teenage son whose problems he cannot (or will not) understand than as "a gracious and tender Father to the penitent" (Martineau's *Common Prayer for Christian Worship*). The implications of this are that instead of preparing Roy for death, by imparting absolution for his sins – his *quia peccavi* ("I've done questionable things") – Tyrell proceeds to draw him back into life by telling him how "extraordinary" he is. Such talk is presumably meant to console him. So limited is his insight into Roy's "mind" – ironic, since he is said by Chew to have "designed" it – that he commends Roy to "revel" in time that he has left on earth. This would be sage advice were it not for the fact that it is too late for that. Without the possibility of a reversal of his termination date, Roy is going to die soon – and there is nothing that he or anyone can do about it.

It is at this point that Roy clasps the head of Tyrell, and, in an Oedipal gesture par excellence, proceeds to gouge his eyes at the same time as using his superhuman strength to crush his skull. Tyrell then "slumps to the floor like empty clothes" (1981 *Blade Runner* script). The son has killed the father; the modern Promethean god of biomechanics is dead, having been killed by his own creation. It is not obvious to me why Roy does this. Not because Roy has no motive to feel resentful toward Tyrell – he does. Like Victor Frankenstein who abandons his creation, Tyrell abandons Roy, whom he has condemned to a life of slavery and premature death. *But the alternative is that Roy would never have been "born."* (It is a separate question as to whether Roy should have been ceded the right to liberty once he was born, but we can assume that this again was out of Tyrell's "jurisdiction.") Roy would have had a legitimate grievance had Roy's short life been so terrible – so deprived and fraught with anxiety – that it would not have been worth living (see Parfit, 1984, ch. 16). But this is clearly not the case. *Roy loves his life, which is why he is doing all he can to extend it.* Roy's killing Tyrell, including the manner in which he kills him, thus appears to be disproportionate to his motive. He will not gain anything by Tyrell's destruction (or Sebastian's, which occurs off scene[5]), even if Tyrell cannot provide him with the solution he is searching for, and so his action seems gratuitous.

The danger here is that Roy's *acte gratuit* risks giving the impression that he is some sort of callous and morally depraved individual. But though Roy, with one important exception, as we will see, kills those who would seek to enslave, appropriate, or "retire" him, he is no psychopath, if by the label is meant a personality disorder characterized by an incapacity for love, loss of insight, unresponsiveness in general interpersonal relations, lack of empathy, and lack of remorse and shame (Cleckley, 1988: 224–25). Roy does not *lack* anything. He, on the contrary, suffers (if that is the right word) from a superabundance of what the Romans called *virtus* shorn of its medieval Christian distortions, and which roughly means "innermost energy" (Giustiniani, 1985: 189). This is indeed how Nietzsche speaks of the Overman – not as someone who is callous, detached, and emotionally shallow, but as someone who says "yes" to life: "I love him whose soul is overfull so that he forgets himself, and all things are in him: thus all things become his downfall" (1978: 16). True, there is an egocentricity to Roy that it serves no purpose to deny. But while that might explain his inadequately motivated antisocial behavior, it does not betoken a pathologic egocentricity. It is in reminding us, without sermons, that there is a more human – or *humane* – disposition to Roy's way of being than that of egocentricity that the value of Scott's movie lies. But we don't get a full sense of this until the showdown with Deckard and his final downfall in the penultimate scene.

Kinship

The battle with Deckard that ensues is the high point of the drama. The whole movie has been for this. It is a battle of wits as much as physical strength. The eloquent, philosophic, and spirited Roy delights in mocking his human-all-too-human opponent, who is outmanned and outmaneuvered:

> Roy: Not very sporting to fire on an unarmed opponent. I thought you were supposed to be good. Aren't you the good man? . . . Proud of yourself, little man? . . . Come on, Deckard, I'm right here, but you've got to shoot straight. . . . Straight doesn't seem to be good enough. . . . You better get it up, or I'm gonna have to kill ya! . . . That was irrational of you. Not to mention unsportsman-like. Ha ha ha. Where are you going?

These are not the words of a man who is determined to kill another. Nothing could be further from ludic Roy's intention, which is to keep the "game" going as long as possible ("One, two. Three, four. . . . [Singing] I'm coming. . . . Four, five. How to stay alive. . . . I can see you! . . . Unless you're alive, you can't play, and if you don't play . . . Six, seven. Go to hell, go to heaven"). After 20 minutes of agon (or cat and mouse!), however, we come to the climax of the movie. An exhausted and terrified Deckard is clinging to the ledge of the Bradbury Building, literally holding on for dear life. Roy stands above him looking down and utters the words: "Quite an experience to live in fear, isn't it? That's what it is to be a slave."[6] It is then, in an unpredictable and heroic act, that Roy expends the last of his vital energy by catching Deckard, who can hold on no longer, and as he does so he exclaims, "Kinship!"

Critics and fans have sought to give various explanations for what is going on here. Why does Roy save Deckard's life? When Hauer asked Scott this question, he reported that Scott told him, "It's pure reflex. Other than that I don't know" (Sammon, 1996: 194). But this can't be right. If Roy were acting purely instinctually, without reflection, then it would destroy the conditions of intelligibility of the word "kinship," which is clearly a meaningful utterance and not merely a groan or expression of exertion. Some have found in this word evidence that Deckard was a replicant after all, an hypothesis that gains plausibility once we recognize that Scott himself seems to have wanted us to think that (despite the fact that he claims not to impute any meaning to the action that attends the utterance!). However, I would suggest a slightly different reading, inspired in large part by the oft-quoted words of the metaphysical poet John Donne:

> No man is an Island, entire of itself; every man is a piece of the Continent, a part of the main; . . . any man's death diminishes me, because I am involved in Mankind; And therefore never send to know for whom the bell tolls; It tolls for thee.
>
> (*Meditation* XVII)

By "kinship," I submit, Roy is calling attention to the fact that both of them – android and human – "have a lot in common"; and that is the impending nature of death itself. It makes little difference that one is human and the other android. Their affinity to one another is not explained by a common physical makeup. They are involved in "mankind" because they can *die*. Both beings find kinship in dying together.

In dying, Roy comes face-to-face with Deckard, who is likewise menaced by death, but also whose death can be postponed by an act of "kinship" – a word that is etymologically connected to "kindness." The face-to-face scene at the end of the movie is one of the most memorable, touching, and ethically charged scenes in the film. The philosopher Mark Rowlands calls it "perhaps the most moving death soliloquy in cinematic history" (Rowlands, 2003: 235). Roy is half-naked, sitting in a lotus position in the pouring rain on the roof of the Bradbury Building, clutching a dove. He stares at Deckard, who is staring back at him attentively, and begins his swan-song:

> Roy: I've seen things you people wouldn't believe. Attack ships on fire off the shoulder of Orion. I watched c-beams glitter in the dark near Tannhäuser Gate. All those moments will be lost in time like tears in rain. Time to die.

What gives impressiveness to these celebratory and memorializing words is that they are Roy's last. Upon his uttering them, he smiles, drops his head – and dies. The kind of consummation that his death brings gratifies our sense of ceremony and our insistence that one's death should be a reflection of the way one lives one's life. *He died as he had lived.*

But the point of the death scene – and this I think is too often neglected in the frequent discussions of it – is not to provide additional evidence for "extraordinary things" that Roy has done or to attest to the superiority of the replicants in general, nor is it to underscore the affinity between replicants and humans – but rather it is to address the question (as Tolstoy put it): "Is there any meaning in my life that will not be destroyed by my inevitably approaching death?" (1996: 35) Although frequently – but, I think, unfairly – criticized as bathos, Deckard's narrative voice-over[7] at the end of the scene quite reasonably suggests an answer to the enigma as to why Roy saved Deckard's life in spite of his own (Roy's) impending death:

> Deckard (voice-over): I don't know why he saved my life. *Maybe in those last moments he loved life more than he ever had before. Not just his life, anybody's*

> *life, my life.* All he'd wanted were the same answers the rest of us want. Where did I come from? Where am I going? How long have I got? All I could do was sit there and watch him die.

What this narration does is divert our attention away from looking at Roy's internal relation to his death, and to his external relations with others that confer on it a meaning and which account for his finally coming to accept his mortality. For we come back to the question as to why Roy should save the life of the man who has been trying to hunt him down and kill him, *a man whose last act just as he fell (before he was caught by Roy) was to spit at Roy in the face.*

The original screenwriter Hampton Fancher has gone on record as saying that Scott believed that this "last, defiant, life affirming gesture" on the part of Deckard is the reason why Roy saves him. Roy "appreciated" Deckard's "spitting in the face of death" (Sammon, 1996: 194). Fortunately, we can avoid this kind of arbitrary (and frankly silly) construction by seeing in Roy's gesture an answer to the question posed a moment ago: "Is there any meaning in my life that will not be destroyed by my inevitable approaching death?" If Roy *had not* saved Deckard's life, if he had merely let him fall to his death and then dragged himself off to some secluded spot on the roof of the Bradbury Building, like a mortally wounded animal, then I think we should have to say that his death on the heels of Deckard's would have been meaningless. Not that he needed witnesses or an audience to view his final curtain and catch the last line of his soliloquy, as though value or meaning depended on the subjective interpretations of others. For Roy to find a meaning in life that will not be washed away by death, his death has to be *caused* in a specific way. *The death must result from dying for another.*

To help us understand the type of thing I am gesturing toward it may help us to recall what Levinas says about how the possibility exists of a meaning that death cannot efface:

> This is why death cannot drain all meaning from life. . . . The will, already betrayal and alienation of itself but postponing this betrayal, on the way to death but a death ever future, exposed to death but not *immediately*, has time to be for the Other, and thus to recover meaning despite death. This existence for the Other, this Desire of

> the other, this goodness liberated from the egoist gravitation, nonetheless retains a personal character. The being thus defined has its time at its disposal precisely because it postpones violence, that is, because a meaningful order subsists beyond death, and thus all the possibilities of discourse are not reduced to desperate blows on a head struck against the wall.
>
> (1969: 236)

Until the rooftop scene, Roy had been reduced to banging his head against a brick wall, both figuratively and literally. (Not only was he frustrated in his quest to extend his life, mad ["batty"] Roy ambuscades Deckard by putting his head through the wall on the Bradbury Building.) Roy's transformation in his relation to his own death comes when, in lifting Deckard from the ledge and saving his life, he is no longer preoccupied with his own life. I assume that this act cost him his life by sapping all but the last of his already depleted vital energy, as evidenced by his nearly falling asleep moments earlier while climbing out of the window. To be sure, Roy is going to die soon even if he does not save Deckard, *but then the right circumstances for his death would never have arisen*. Doesn't Roy's sacrifice exemplify the sort of phenomenon to which Levinas is referring when he speaks of "goodness liberated from the egoist gravitation"? This is how we can make sense of the obscure conviction that the final moments of Roy's life are not like the other moments that will be "lost in time" ("c-beams glittering in the dark," etc., etc.), and which are not just unique but uniquely meaningful inasmuch as they make possible a future that *is not Roy's but which counts for Roy* – something

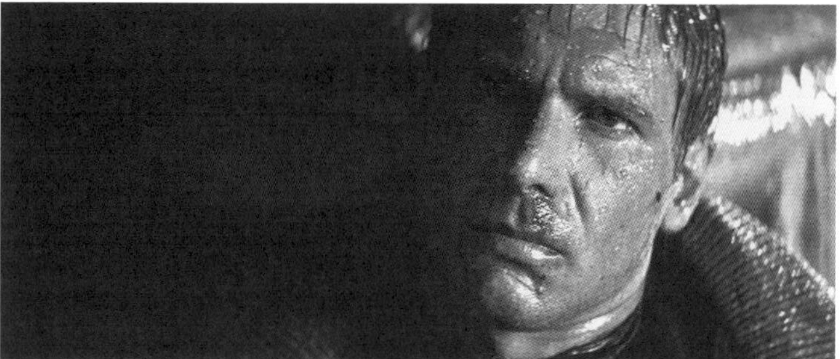

Figure 3.2 Still from *Blade Runner* (Theatrical Cut) Dir. Ridley Scott (1982)

that can't be rationally justified but which everybody who is concerned about posterity understands.

Dying with

I wish to draw attention briefly to one other aspect about death in *Blade Runner* before departing. It concerns the role of the witness at the moment of dying. For the most part the witnesses to the many deaths that appear on-screen are bystanders, in that they have no relation to the one who is dying. They do not intervene in such a way as to try to prevent the death, nor does their presence in any way attend to the one who is dying. This is obviously true of the street people who watch Zhora as she is killed by Deckard,[8] but it is no less true of Sebastian as he watches Tyrell's murder. The only exception here is Deckard silently watching Roy die. He says in the post-mortem voice-over: "All I could do was sit there and watch him die." But this claim conceals as much as it reveals. Deckard may not say anything verbal to Roy, but Roy is addressing himself to Deckard, whose very *presence* amounts to a response of sorts. What is that response that is different from that of the bystander who just looks on at the spectacle that the dying other presents? The response of the one who is there lying on a rooftop in the rain is no different from that of the hospice worker who is sitting beside the bed of the dying person – *it is not to let the person who is dying die alone*. This constitutes an implicit challenge to the Heideggerian description of death as something that is non-relational inasmuch as death is the one possibility that I cannot in principle have someone else live for me. Although there is an obvious sense in which this is true, it is equally the case – and Scott's film shows this better than any other film I know – that a "social conjuncture is maintained in this menace" (Levinas, 1969: 234). Deckard, having been saved from death by Roy, reciprocates by not leaving Roy alone with the mystery of death. It is as though Roy's death were not solely Roy's *business*, but Deckard's too. "Business" here no longer refers to the retirement of replicants (earlier in the film Deckard had explained that the tremors he experienced after killing a replicant was "part of the business"), but is to be understood in the sense of *concern*. Roy's transformation in his relation to his death thus brings about a transformation in Deckard. The man whose ex-wife called him "sushi" ("cold fish") has had kindled in him a compassionate concern for the person who is dying, and in so doing displays his own humanity.

Conclusion

Ridley Scott's film *Blade Runner* is unabashedly philosophical. Its questions include questions about the nature of what is human: "Where did I come from? Where am I going? How long have I got?" More original than this triumvirate, however, is the question which lies at the very core of the film: "What if?" *What if the replicants are also human?* (The lesser canvas – What if Deckard is a replicant? – is, I have suggested, uninteresting in comparison.) By focusing on the character of Roy Batty I have tried to show that replicants express their humanity insofar as their lives are lived in the Heideggerian sense of being-toward-death. In Scott's film, it is Roy's dying that discloses truly human possibilities, which include not only a joyful celebration of life, a great "yes" to life and concomitant "no" to death, but also the distinctly human possibility of salvaging a meaning from life that impending death cannot efface; indeed, without that meaning, which is highlighted by Roy's saving Deckard's life, the film would not have the ingredients to answer its own question about how the replicants in the film paradoxically surpass the humanity even of those who create them.[9] The exception here is Deckard, whose role as witness to Roy's death permits him to express his own humanity in the form of not leaving Roy alone with the mystery of death.[10] Ironically it is he and he alone among the non-replicants in the film[11] who *recognizes* the humanity of the replicants. True, he has not seen what Roy has seen, and he cannot experience what Roy is experiencing as he watches him die. But despite this cognitive mismatch we do see *how* he is emotionally affected by the death of one of those whom it is his job to "retire." And in this way Deckard shows us what true empathy looks like.[12]

Roy leaves most of the audience with the profound impression of the ephemeral nature of life and human experience, already anticipated by Lucretius, the Roman poet and philosopher from the first century BCE, and quoted by Montaigne in his *Essays*, I, 20:

> *Jam fuerit, nec post unquam revocare licebit.*
>
> (*De Rerum Natura*, III, 195; quoted by Montaigne, 1993: 25)

"The present will soon be past, never to be recalled." And it is perhaps the strength of this impression that makes *Blade Runner* such a memorable film. But what I think makes it a great film is not just that it seems capable of competing successfully with philosophy in providing an understanding of human nature and death. The scenes it depicts may serve functions similar to those addressed in a philosophical treatise like *Being and Time*, but they also do something more. They show up the dismal contrast between two worlds: the world of lifeless mechanism, in which most humans left on earth are at home, and a conception of nature as something not essentially inert or robotic, but fruitful and capable of finding a meaning in life despite the inevitable death that awaits.

Notes

1 The *Domestic Cut* (original 1982 American Theatrical Release).

2 The first thing Roy says to Chew upon entering the Eye Works is: "Fiery the Angels fell, / Deep thunder rolled around their shores, / Burning with the fires of Orc."

The lines are a deliberate misquote of Blake's allegorical poem "America: A Prophesy," about American revolutionaries fighting in the colonies for freedom ("Fiery the Angels rose, & as they rose deep thunder roll'd / Around their shores: indignant burning with the fires of Orc.") The substitution of "fell" for "rose" clearly shows that Roy sees himself and the other rogue replicants not so much as revolutionary angels rising above tyranny in the "Off-world colonies" (the film's crawl informs us that replicants were used as slave labor in the perilous exploration and colonization of other planets), but as Miltonic fallen angels "Hurl'd headlong flaming from th' Ethereal Sky" (*Paradise Lost*, Book I: 45). For a discussion of Blakean–Miltonic overtones in *Blade Runner*, see Harley (2005).

3 Following a suggestion by Harley (2005: 69).

4 This line, which occurs in the *Domestic Cut* (1982) and the *Director's Cut* (1993), is changed in the *Final Cut* (2007) to the more urbane "I want more life, father," with its Oedipal/Frankensteinian overtones.

5 The fact that Roy kills Sebastian for no apparent reason is one of the film's many inconsistencies. Roy has no reason to kill Sebastian, who has helped him get to Tyrell, who poses no threat to him or Pris. One suspects that the writers simply needed a pretext for Deckard – who hears about the death of Sebastian on the police radio – to visit Sebastian's apartment.

6 We do not have to treat these words as a continuation of his mocking from earlier. The fear of death is an experience that Roy knows all too well. Man or android we all serve what Hegel dubbed the "absolute master" (1977: 361).

7 It should be noted that the voice-over occurs in the *Domestic Cut* but not in the *Director's Cut* or the *Final Cut*. Also, the voice-over was apparently neither written nor approved by Scott (see Sammon, 1996: 351), but was added by the studio in post-production.

8 Deckard appears to be the only one moved by Zhora's death, which he considers *homicide*: "The report would be routine retirement of a replicant which didn't make me feel any better about shooting a woman [sic] in the back."

9 I say "film" because the being-toward-death that constitutes the essence of the replicants' humanity is clearly not what the Tyrell Corporation has in mind in its motto "more human than human." This is because replicants were "designed to copy human beings in every way except their emotions." Being emotionless, replicants would be incapable of experiencing the basic emotional state or mood of anxiety that characterizes being-toward-death in general.

10 It might be retorted that Deckard has no choice in the matter. Since he was injured and exhausted from the battle he had just fought (and lost), he wasn't able to go anywhere. But this is superficial and not nearly enough to explain the emotional state – which is no longer fear – expressed on Deckard's face as he abandons the role of adversary and adopts that of witness to Roy's dying last moments.

11 To prevent misunderstandings let me add that I am not adjudicating the issue of whether Deckard is a replicant. I am simply assuming that he is not, as did most people associated with the film at the time of its original theatrical release, including the film's screenwriters (though not Scott himself it later appears [Sammon, 1996: 359–64; 390–92]). I agree that there are grounds to go either way on this issue, and that my assumption is therefore susceptible to being challenged. At any rate, the point is that the above argument – that the humanity of the replicants lies in their being mortal – is perfectly compatible with the interpretation of Deckard as a replicant. If anything, it helps it, since it is probably true that if replicants have an acute awareness of their own mortality they have the capacity to empathize with the anxiety and suffering of others who also are dying.

12 I am pleased to be able to express my gratitude for the comments and inspiration I received from students and faculty in the Philosophy Department, California State University Fullerton, where I delivered an earlier version of this paper.

References

Bernasconi, R. (2000) "Whose Death Is It Anyway? Philosophy and the Cultures of Death" in *Khoraographies for Jacques Derrida Tympanum* 4, available online at www.usc.edu/dept/comp-lit/tympanum/4/bernasconi.html.

Cleckley, H. (1988) *The Mask of Sanity*, St. Louis, MO: Mosby.

Desser, D. (1991) "The New Eve: The Influence of *Paradise Lost* and *Frankenstein* on *Blade Runner*" in *Retrofitting Blade Runner: Issues in Ridley Scott's Blade Runner and Philip K. Dick's Do Androids Dream of Electric Sheep?*, ed. J. B. Kerman, Bowling Green, OH: Bowling Green State University Popular Press, 53–65.

de Waal, F. (2009) *The Age of Empathy*, New York: Harmony Books.

Giustiniani, V. R. (1985) "Homo, Humanus, and the Meanings of 'Humanism,'" *Journal of the History of Ideas*, vol. 46, no. 2, 167–95.

Harley, A. (2005) "America, a Prophecy: When Blake Meets *Blade Runner*," *Sydney Studies in English*, vol. 31, 61–75.

Hegel, G. W. F. (1977) *Phenomenology of Spirit*, trans. A. V. Miller, Oxford: Clarendon Press.

Heidegger, M. (1962) *Being and Time*, trans. J. Macquarrie and E. Robinson, Oxford: Basil Blackwell.

—— (1971) "Building Dwelling Thinking" in *Poetry, Language, Thought*, trans. A. Hofstadter, New York: Harper and Row.

Hemingway, E. (1960) *Death in the Afternoon*, New York: Scribner.

Kaufmann, W. (1974) *Nietzsche: Philosopher, Psychologist, Antichrist*, Princeton, NJ: Princeton University Press.

Kierkegaard, S. (1967) *Journals and Papers*, vol. 1, ed. and trans. H. V. Hong and E. H. Hong, Bloomington, IN: Indiana University Press.

Levinas, E. (1969) *Totality and Infinity*, trans. A. Lingis, Pittsburgh: Duquesne University Press.

—— (1987) *Time and the Other*, trans. R. A. Cohen, Pittsburgh: Duquesne University Press.

Montaigne, M. de (1993) *Essays: A Selection*, trans. M. A. Screech, London: Penguin.

Nietzsche, F. (1978) *Thus Spoke Zarathustra*, trans. W. Kaufmann, New York: Penguin.

Parfit, D. (1984) *Reasons and Persons*, Oxford: Oxford University Press.

Rowlands, M. (2003) *The Philosopher at the End of the Universe*, New York: Random House.

Sammon, P. M. (1996) *Future Noir: The Making of Blade Runner*, New York: HarperCollins.

Shapiro, M. J. (1993) "'Manning' the Frontiers: The Politics of (Human) Nature in Blade Runner" in *In the Nature of Things: Language, Politics, and the Environment*, ed. J. Bennett and W. Chaloupka, Minneapolis: University of Minnesota Press, 65–84.

Tolstoy, L. (1996) *Confession*, trans. D. Patterson, New York: W. W. Norton.

Chapter 4

C. D. C. Reeve

REPLICANT LOVE

BLADE RUNNER VOIGHT-KAMPFFED

IT IS NOVEMBER 2019 and we are in the Los Angeles of Ridley Scott's *Blade Runner: The Director's Cut* (1992). Out of the vast industrial cityscape, an enormous Mayan-temple-like building comes into view. It is the Tyrell Corporation and its business is manufacturing Replicants – products "designed to copy human beings in every way except their emotions." The reason for the exception is soon clear. Pris is "a basic pleasure model. A standard item for military clubs in the out colonies." Imagine what it would be like if she had a rich array of human feelings. Or if Zhora, "trained for an off-world kick murder squad," did. Or Roy Batty, a "combat model" designed for "optimum self-sufficiency." With complex systems, though, you never know what they will do, given enough time: "The designers reckoned that after a few years, they might develop their own emotional responses. Hate, love, fear, anger, envy. So they built in a fail-safe device . . . Four-year lifespan."[1]

There they are, then, these short-lived Replicants, impassively and slavishly doing our degrading and violent dirty work far away in space. And what happens? They do develop emotions. Angry, envious, filled with hatred, and maybe in love with Pris, Roy leads her, Zhora, and Leon in revolt. They slaughter twenty-three people, jump a shuttle back to Earth, and head for the Tyrell Corporation. True, they will all self-destruct before long. Roy's "incept date" is 2016, Leon's is April 17, 2017. In the meantime, what they are is a problem.

That's where Blade Runners come in. A police squad trained to detect and "retire" Replicants who return to Earth, they are the first line of defense against the "machines" humans have made to be their slaves. The question is, will it be effective against those of the Nexus 6 generation, like Batty and the others? Maybe the detection method – the so-called Voight-Kampff test – won't work on them. Maybe Blade Runners won't be up to the task of "airing them out." When Holden, who is supposed to be good, runs into Leon, now an employee at Tyrell, he is the one that ends up on the critical list – "He can breathe okay, as long as nobody unplugs him." In desperation, Bryant, the squad leader, calls in the retired Rick Deckard. "This is a bad one. The worst yet. I need the old Blade Runner. I need your magic." It's a flattering appeal, but Deckard is deaf to it. Even he is daunted by what he would face. "I was quit when I came in here Bryant," he says. "I'm twice as quit now." In the end, he has to be threatened to comply. "You know the score, pal. You're not cop, you're little people."

It is a threat that the whole atmosphere of the film makes real. "Is that why you're still on Earth?" Pris asks J. F. Sebastian, a genetic designer for Tyrell, when she learns he has a glandular disorder that ages him prematurely. "Yeah," he replies. "I couldn't pass the medical." We may be in the future, but we are not in the socially desirable part of it – the good neighborhood. Earth seems to have become one vast polluted industrial park, on which a brown drizzle endlessly falls. The owners and managers, like Eldon Tyrell, live high above it all, as close to off-world as they can get, while the workers (who for the most part really are little people) scurry around on crowded streets, under the ever-watchful eye of the authorities and their cameras. There is no visible vegetation. Natural species are largely extinct. "Do you think I'd be working in a place like this," Zhora asks Deckard, "if I could afford a *real* snake?" Even cows are so rare that calfskin wallets are illegal. High culture, too, seems to have disappeared. What's left is Asian fast food from street vendors, artificial pets for those who can afford the high prices, and striptease and strong liquor at Taffy Lewis's. Sure, it's the demimonde typical of *film noir*, but it is also the wasteland Earth has become under human stewardship.

"Is this to be an empathy test?" Tyrell asks Deckard, when Deckard is sent by Bryant to see if Voight-Kampff does work on a Nexus 6. "Capillary dilation of the so-called blush response? Fluctuation of the pupil. Involuntary dilation of the iris . . . I want to see it work on a person.

I want to see a negative before I provide you with a positive." His candidate is Rachael. After a hundred or more questions (the normal is twenty or thirty), Tyrell sends her out of the room. Deckard, he sees, is coming to the conclusion that she is actually a positive.

> Deckard: She doesn't know?
> Tyrell: She's beginning to suspect, I think.
> Deckard: Suspect! How can it not know what it is?

Tyrell's answer is revelatory – and in a way other than that intended.

> Commerce is our goal here at Tyrell. "More human than human" is our motto. Rachael is an experiment. Nothing more. We began to recognize in them a strange obsession. After all, they are emotionally inexperienced, with only a few years to store up the experiences which you and I take for granted. If we gift them with a past, we create a cushion or a pillow for their emotions and consequently we can control them better.

Tyrell has not been keeping the police informed, we see, about Nexus 6s. What for Bryant is only a designer's projection – a maybe – is for Tyrell a certainty. Replicants not only develop emotions, they do it so quickly that a cushion is needed in addition to a fail-safe device. If the magnificent artificial owl presiding over Tyrell's office aerie is very expensive, what must Rachael or Pris or Roy Batty cost? Commercial viability requires a degree of longevity in a product – an adequate shelf life. But longevity comes with liabilities, which need then to be offset – cushioned. The business of the US in 2019 may still be business, but the tensions between commercial interests and the commonweal are as real as ever.

"Memories," Deckard responds. "You're talking about memories." Well, *quasi-memories*[2] anyway – elements with a role in a Replicant's psychology like that of actual memories in a human's, but with an important difference. When I remember my first piano lesson, a causal chain connects the memory experience to the lesson via my perceptions of it. That's what makes it both a memory (rather than a fantasy) and mine. When Rachael "remembers" her first piano lesson, on the other hand, or playing doctor with her brother in an empty building, or the spider outside her bedroom window that gets eaten by its own babies, there are no causal links to her own past perceptions of these events. "Those aren't your memories," Deckard tells her. "They're somebody else's. They're Tyrell's niece's." They're "implants." Nevertheless, just as my sense of myself, of who and what I am, is a precipitate of my memories, so Rachael's is a precipitate of her quasi-memories. And what they tell her – like what her mirror and the reactions of others tell her – is that she's a human being. Had she been "gifted" with the superhuman strength, speed, and resilience of Batty, or the acrobatic skills and heat tolerance of Pris, the story might have been different. Rachael, however, wasn't designed for off-world dirty work. That's why she is a lot more like us than the others – a lot more human. Though it is implied that she is a Nexus 6, there is room for doubt about whether she really is one, and not some yet newer model. Batty and the others have four-year lifespans, but does she? It is important to the film that the question be left hanging.

"What do they risk coming back to Earth for?" Deckard asks Bryant as he is being briefed on Nexus 6s. "That's unusual. What do they want out of the Tyrell Corporation?" Quasi-memories answer both his questions. The emotional cushion or pillow they provide, as we see from the photographs Leon and Rachael both carry around like talismans, is a sense of home and family, of being loved and cherished, and the sense of self that comes with it. Nexus 6s return to the Tyrell Corporation for the same sorts of reasons we return home. And they are expected. "I'm surprised you didn't come here sooner," Tyrell tells Batty, when the two are at last face to face. "It's not an easy thing to meet your maker," he replies.

The ambiguity is intentional. Tyrell is a mixture of our earthly biological fathers and what we find it natural to call our heavenly father – God. At home, we are comforted and revitalized – reassured about who we are – by contact with the loving people and dear places of our childhood memories, precisely because they *are* the people and places of our childhood:

> There is no sense of ease like the ease we felt in those scenes where we were born, where objects had become dear to us before we had known the labour of choice, and where the outer world seemed only an extension of our own personality: we accepted and loved it as

> we loved and accepted our own sense of existence and our own limbs. Very commonplace, even ugly, that furniture of our early home might look if it were put up to auction; an improved taste in upholstery scorns it; and is not the striving after something better and better in our surroundings the grand characteristic that distinguishes man from the brute? . . . But heaven knows where that striving might lead us, if our affections had not a trick of twining round those old familiar things – if the loves and sanctities of our life had no deep immovable roots in memory. One's delight in an elderberry bush overhanging the confused leafage of a hedgerow bank, as a more gladdening sight than the finest cistus or fuchsia spreading itself on the softest undulating turf, is an entirely unjustifiable preference to a nursery-gardener, or to any of those severely regulated minds who are free from the weakness of any attachment that does not rest on a demonstrable superiority of qualities. And there is no better reason for preferring this elderberry bush than that it stirs an early memory – that it is no novelty in my life, speaking to me merely through my present sensibilities to form and colour, but the long companion of my existence, that wove itself into my joys when joys were vivid.[3]

When Batty says, "I want more life . . . Father," however, it isn't revitalizing and reassuring George Eliot-esque contact with vivid joys that he seeks. What he wants is what God alone can grant – the conquest of death. But death, as Tyrell admits, is "a little out of my jurisdiction."

We don't blame our fathers for not making us immortal. We know it isn't in their gift. We don't blame them for not giving us the genetic means to the greatest possible human life expectancy. That isn't theirs to give either (not yet, anyway). When Tyrell says that the "light that burns twice as bright, burns half as long. And you have burned so very brightly, Roy," we see the pertinence. The measure of a life's value is not its length alone. When Tyrell goes on to say, "You were made as well as we could make you," however, Batty is not deceived. "But *not to last*," he replies. A genetic "coding sequence" may indeed be unchangeable "*after* it has been established," but that doesn't mean that it could not have been established to code for a longer lifespan in the first place. Cold behind his thick, oversized glasses, Tyrell is impassive in the face of Batty's plight. Fatherly love isn't part of his equation.

Trading stocks on the phone in the small hours, it is all commerce with him.

"I ought to be thy Adam," the creature Victor Frankenstein has created says to him, "but I am rather the fallen angel, whom thou drivest from joy for no misdeed . . . I was benevolent and good; misery made me a fiend."[4] He has been made a fiend not by scalpel and electricity, but by lack of a father's love. When Batty transforms William Blake's line "Fiery the angels rose" into "Fiery the angels *fell*," it is with this poor creature turned fiend that he identifies. When he realizes or confirms the grim truth about how and why he has been made as he is (he already knows about incept dates and longevity), he takes Tyrell's head between his hands, kisses him passionately on the mouth, and crushes his skull. The high wages of single-minded commercialism have been exacted. It is a nice irony that the poem from which Blake's line comes is "America, a Prophecy."

Judas betrayed Jesus to the Jewish and (ultimately) Roman authorities with a similarly passionate kiss.[5] Like that kiss, Batty's leads to the death of someone in whom both divine and human elements are mixed. To try to harm the divine, the source of all goodness, is Satanic. "Evil, be thou my good," Milton's Satan says.[6] When Batty kills Chew, who designed his eyes, and Sebastian, who tried to help him, it is of that other fiery fallen angel that we are reminded. We smell brimstone. Because Tyrell is neither God nor good, however, another odor is also present when he is killed – not of sanctity, to be sure, but of something sweet, all the same. Genius or not, Tyrell is very hard to like.

In the final exchange between father and son, with its biblical allusions and reference to heaven, the issue of immortality is subtly linked to those of freedom and moral responsibility.

Tyrell: You're the prodigal son. You're quite a prize.
Batty: I've done questionable things.
Tyrell: Also extraordinary things. Revel in your time.
Batty: Nothing the god of bio-mechanics wouldn't let you in heaven for.

Is he talking about himself? Maybe, he is. But he is also surely talking about Tyrell. The questionable things I, Batty, have done, he is saying, *you*, Tyrell, are responsible for, since you made me. Were we to bring a similar charge against our divine maker, he would respond, theologians tell us, by reminding us of our immortal souls and the freedom of will they enjoy as not wholly subject to the causal order. A machine or a soulless brute is not free, he would say, because factors over which it has no control determine its choices and actions. A soul is free, because there are no such factors. It can always choose and act otherwise than it does. Since immortal souls are outside his jurisdiction, Tyrell cannot respond in this way to Batty. The cushion quasi-memories provide for Replicant emotions, he says, allows them to be more effectively *controlled*. Perhaps, though, some other response is available. If control of Nexus 6s were perfect, after all, they would still be off-world doing the jobs they were designed to do, and Tyrell wouldn't be having the conversation that leads to his death.

When Rachael is Voight-Kampffed, a third traditional attribute of the soul – self-consciousness – is referred to: "How can it not know what it is?" At one level, the question is answered, as we saw, by the fact that Rachael's implanted memories are those of a human. There is another level involved, however, which only becomes explicit when Replicants discuss themselves:

Batty: We're not computers, Sebastian. We're physical.
Pris: I think, Sebastian, therefore I am.
Batty: Very good, Pris. Now show him why.

In response she does a back-flip and reaches into a flask of boiling water to pull out an egg. These are tricks intended to appeal to the toy-loving Sebastian, whose assistance in reaching Tyrell Pris and Batty are trying to elicit. They are also philosophical jokes. The "I" whose existence Descartes hopes to establish by means of the so-called *Cogito* ("I think, therefore I am") is an entirely mental entity, which cannot perform such feats.[7] The fact remains that Pris seems to be able to establish her existence just as Descartes thinks that we can establish ours. She may not have a soul, but she seems to have the self-consciousness that supposedly comes only with possessing one.

Impressive though this deep similarity between Pris and us undoubtedly is, Batty's instruction points to an equally impressive apparent difference. Pris knows *why* she exists. Her tricks are things she was designed to do, just as Sebastian's toys were designed to welcome him home. Her revealing clothes and sexy body are part of the repertoire of a basic pleasure model. But if Pris is a pleasure model, while Zhora is trained for a kick murder squad, why is it Zhora who is working as a snake dancer in a strip club? Why is it Pris who has the murderous legs? A Replicant's intended purpose, it seems, is one it can subvert. Design is not determining or freedom-destroying. It isn't fate. Replicants can thwart it.

In an extended comic scene, Deckard, masquerading as a representative of the Confidential Committee on Moral Abuses, interviews Zhora about her job. Did she feel exploited in any way by the club's management? To get the job, did she do or was she asked to do "anything that's lewd or unsavory or otherwise repulsive" to her person? Are there, perhaps, "little dirty holes" in her dressing-room walls through which men can watch her undress? "You'd be surprised," he says, "what a guy would go through to get a glimpse of a beautiful body." "No, I wouldn't," is her pointed reply. Zhora got her job, she is all too aware, not because she's a Replicant (no one knows she is one), but because men will pay for the sexual pleasure they get from watching women (real or Replicant) doing degrading things ("watch her take her pleasure from the serpent that once corrupted man"). Economic reality and male domination are not the same thing as universal causal determinism, to be sure, but the threat they pose to freedom is one that the possession of a soul is a poor safeguard against – or no better a safeguard than rebellious Replicant slaves possess.

Though the freedom to which God appeals to defend himself against the charge of being responsible for our evil acts is incompatible with universal determinism, another conception of freedom exists that is compatible with it. Human beings are free, on this conception, not because they have souls that allow them to slip through nature's causal net, or because they can slip through it in some other way, but because they can often do what they want (and so have freedom of action), and also want what they want (and so have freedom of choice or will).[8] And that is all the freedom – defenders of this conception suggest – that is required for responsibility. What difference does it make, they ask, that someone could not have chosen or acted otherwise, if he would have chosen or acted in the same way in any case? Perhaps this is the sort of freedom that is within a Replicant's reach – the sort Tyrell might have appealed to in responding to Batty.

The issue here, to give a name to the relevant aspect of our sense of self, is that of *practical identity*. The will I have, we may suppose, is my own work. I have the wants and desires that cause or motivate the actions I perform because I – on the basis of experience and reflection – want to have them. What they constitute, as a result, is not just *a* will, but *my* will, my practical identity. If Rachael has the wants and desires she does because Tyrell's niece or someone else wanted them, however, the will she has may in some sense be free, but is it really *hers?*

In one scene in particular, the issue of practical identity seems explicitly in focus. Rachael has saved Deckard by shooting Leon and is with him in his apartment. We see him tend to his wounds, then drift off to sleep on the sofa. Rachael looks through the photos on his piano's music stand and begins to play. After a few bars, she stops and seems caught in a reverie. She reaches up and lets down her hair. Deckard awakes and joins her by the piano.

> Deckard: I dreamt music.
> Rachael: I didn't know if I could play. I remember lessons. I don't know if it's me or Tyrell's niece.
> Deckard: You play beautifully.

He kisses her on the cheek and they gaze soulfully into one another's eyes. When he tries to kiss her on the mouth, however, Rachael pulls back. It's as if the doubts she has expressed about her identity as a pianist have made her uncertain about her identity as an agent. Am I the one who wants to return his kiss, her look seems to say, or Tyrell's niece? She becomes agitated and tries to leave. Deckard blocks the doorway and kicks the door shut behind him. He grabs her by the shoulders and pushes her against the wall. There are many more violent scenes in the film, but few that are more disquieting. Then he pulls her to him and kisses her long and hard.

> Deckard: Now you kiss me.
> Rachael: I can't rely on my mem . . .
> Deckard: Say, "kiss me."
> Rachael: Kiss me.

Eventually, she begins to kiss him back. "I want you," he says. Her response is a low, uncertain echo: "I want you." "Again," he says. "I want you," she replies. This time her voice is stronger, the line seems hers, not his. Finally, she seems to speak entirely for herself, "Put your hands on me," she says. Ventriloquism no longer seems a live issue.

Rachael can play the piano. She can read music and strike the right notes. But does she do it as *she* would do it – expressing her own feelings, her own style – or as Tyrell's niece would? It is an odd sort of question, to be sure, but the film helps us give it sense. The way she is shown as first echoing Deckard and then more fully inhabiting her words and actions is emotionally convincing. Yet the question about her piano playing threatens our conviction. Ventriloquism may no longer *seem* to be an issue, but on what grounds exactly are we excluding it?

Physical pain has the capacity, apparently, to cut through the veneer of practical identity to what lies beneath.[9] When Deckard pushes her against the wall, the pain Rachael feels is hers not Tyrell's niece's and nothing about memories can change that. Some sorts of pleasure may seem to have the same capacity – the pleasure of orgasm, for example, or of sexual excitement. The fact that Rachael becomes visibly more turned on as she comes to speak and act with greater apparent autonomy suggests that the film is trading in such ideas – intimating that a practical identity, previously questionable, can find in erotic love an authenticity which cannot be gainsaid by memory implants. That love can give the self a new center of gravity and lead us to remake our will is almost a commonplace. As the love of our parents gave us life, so our later loves can, within limits, make our life anew. What we see in the scene is the beginning of a new love, but also – we are invited to think – of new lives, new wills.

It is an invitation that we, as gluttons for love stories with happy endings, want to accept. Yet the film has again put obstacles in our way. Puzzled and upset after her Voight-Kampff test, Rachael goes to Tyrell. He refuses to see her. To him, as we know, she is "an experiment. Nothing more." To her, he seems much more than that – not a father, perhaps, but an admired employer, or a dear uncle, or something along those lines. In turmoil about her nature and sense of who or what she is, we can imagine her turning to her own memories and memorabilia for the comfort and reassurance he has denied her: "This is me with my mother." Then she visits Deckard and discovers that her memories and memorabilia are fakes. Not only does Tyrell not care about her, her loving mother never existed. She isn't loved by her now and was never loved by her.

Our mother's loving gaze and gentle touch, her suckling breast, her comforting embrace – all these are the life's blood of our emerging self and our sense of it. What pleasure and pain are for us is never – or never for long – simply a somatic matter. An inadequate mother may weave a thread of masochism into us, so that pain and love become knit together. Or she may weave in a different thread, one that makes pleasure of a certain sort crucial. As we develop and mature, we find, as a result, that nothing counts as love for us unless it involves violence or criticism or withholding or tantalization. This is, so to speak, the deep structure of our style of loving and being loved, like the personal style of a good pianist or a city's distinctive sense of place (the *there* that's there). In an intimate relationship it – usually unconsciously – is what is in operation. What, if anything, we must wonder, plays this role in Rachael? If the answer is nothing, what does that imply about her? Is the new practical identity she is forming in falling in love with Deckard somehow compromised? Is it not really *hers* because it lacks a basis in a self that is certified, so to speak, by a mother's love? The film doesn't answer these questions, but it does allow them to cast a shadow of doubt on our romantic wishes for Deckard and Rachael.

When I feel empathy toward you, I stand in your shoes and *replicate* your thoughts and feelings. If I am good at it, I may be able to sense what is really going on with you in a way that even you yourself cannot. Thoughts and feelings are often inchoate and deeply buried. We don't always know what we are thinking or feeling. Sympathetic lovers can be a few steps ahead of us. They can know what is up with us when we are still in the dark. A good mother is like that with her child – sometimes, disconcertingly, even when he is grown up. We can disguise our thoughts and feelings, too, and often have to. The child's candor and guilelessness need to be replaced with adult discretion and discrimination. I don't *feel* grateful, but it would be callous not to at least pretend to be. I think your new dress is hideous, but it would be cruel not to dissimulate. To sustain our privacy we must sometimes hide, sometimes lie.

Most dissimulators are not skilled actors, so we can often see through them. We are quite good at detecting run-of-the-mill liars and fakes. Replicants, however, are not dissimulators. They aren't putting on an act. Their empathic or emotional responses to the scenarios Voight-Kampff deploys are sincere. There is a level of response, however, indicated by blushing, fluctuation of the pupil, involuntary dilation of the iris, that lies deeper than not just their capacity to simulate, but than anything that they could possibly have in their emotional repertoire, given their short lives and emotional inexperience. Voight-Kampff isn't, as it may at first seem, a lie detector test, or a test for moral sentiments. It is more like a brief psychoanalytic session. We are clued into this at the beginning of the film when Holden is Voight-Kampffing Leon:

Holden: Describe in single words only the good things that come into your mind about your mother.
Leon: My mother?
Holden: Yeah.
Leon: I'll tell you about my mother. (He pulls out a gun and shoots Holden.)

But while psychoanalytic sessions explore an unconscious that is known to be there – a dark impress that is a residue of infantile experience and natural constitution – Voight-Kampff tests for the presence of an unconscious, and for the fine structure of feeling it betokens. Testing for it, as a result, is testing for the right sort of thing, given the aim. When Rachael fails the test, therefore, she fails something that relates to her capacity to really empathize and love, and that has consequences for our own romantic wishes for her and Deckard.

When we next see Deckard after his love scene with Rachael, he is parked in his car listening to Bryant telling him about the deaths of Tyrell and Sebastian. Replicant love may have taken root in him but for now at least he is still the old Blade Runner, still in what he calls "the business." At Bryant's command, he is soon in Sebastian's apartment, his head being crushed between Pris's legs. When he manages to shoot her, her limbs thrash about so rapidly in her death throes that she seems more like a weird insect or an electric toy gone haywire than a human. The contrast with Batty's apparently noble and all-too-human end seems intentional. In deciding what to make of it, we are forced to factor Pris's death into our decision. Would Batty thrash around insect-like, too, if his short life hadn't simply run its course – if his battery hadn't, so to speak, run down? Is he "like us" or not? As in the case of the romance between Deckard and Rachael, the film seems bent on preventing us from taking the easy way out.

"I have seen things you people wouldn't believe," Batty says as he breathes his last. "Attack ships on fire off the shoulder of Orion. I watched C-beams glitter in the dark near the Tannhäuser Gate. All those moments will be lost in time like tears in rain." Indeed, they will. If the reason Batty wants more life is to prevent their loss, only immortality will serve his purpose. Immortality may not be something Tyrell can give, but implicitly, at least, it is what Batty seems in the end to have really wanted from him. When the philosopher Friedrich Schlegel writes that only "in relation to the infinite is there meaning and purpose,"[10] he speaks for much of philosophy and religion, but also it seems for Roy Batty. He speaks, too, for something deep inside all of us to which philosophy and religion give expression. We want to be immortal because we think that unless we are, nothing – not even ourselves – can have any ultimate value. Death devalues everything. Whether invented, discovered, or revealed, the soul is a relative of that deep-seated want.

That we humans have souls, we are confident. That mere brutes and mere machines do not, we are confident, too. Our value is assured; theirs, undermined or in jeopardy. What happens to us matters; what happens to them does not. Airing-out or retiring a Replicant, like slaughtering a cow or any other soulless brute, may be harder to watch than switching off a computer or unplugging a television set, but from the point of view of ultimate value, what is the difference? We can do what we like to the soulless. It is some such view, the film suggests, that explains the treatment meted out to Replicants by human beings. As Batty dies, the white dove he has been holding is released and flies off skyward. Traditionally an emblem of the soul leaving the body, it is here only a freed bird – and a wry comment on human values and what underwrites them.

In a short paper entitled "On Transience," written in 1916 in the midst of World War I, Sigmund Freud writes about a young poet with whom he once took a walk in the countryside:

> The poet admired the beauty of the scene around us but felt no joy in it. He was disturbed by the thought that all this beauty was fated to extinction, that it would vanish when winter came, like all human

> beauty and all the beauty and splendour that men have created or may create. All that he would otherwise have loved and admired seemed to him to be shorn of its worth by the transience which was its doom.

The poet, like Saint Augustine in his *Confessions*, thinks that only what cannot perish is worthy of love, so he refuses to love anything mortal. Freud is not convinced that this response is justified. Transience does not involve loss of worth, he thinks, but rather an increase: "Transience value is scarcity value in time. Limitation in the possibility of an enjoyment raises the value of the enjoyment."[11]

Whether we are convinced by Freud in this regard or not, we are even less likely to be convinced by the poet or the saint. Our love for things is independent of any beliefs we may have about their immortality. We love others before we know what they are or how long they will last. We are invested in advance and cannot withdraw our investment when we discover just how high the stakes are. We may believe that the ones we love are as immortal as we, but that may provide less comfort than we are typically inclined to think. First, we cannot ensure their salvation rather than their damnation, so that eternal separation – and with a cruel twist – may be our lot anyway. We cannot ensure the eternity of their love, so that even if they go on forever in the same place as ourselves their love for us may not last. Love is mortal, even if lovers themselves are not. By making itself a love story, therefore, the film seems to side with mortality, with change.

When Deckard initially refuses to help with the Nexus 6s, Bryant's strange lieutenant, Gaff, places a small paper chicken on the desk. Later, when Deckard finds in Leon's shower drain an artificial snake scale that leads him to Zhora, Gaff makes a matchstick man with what seems to be a large erection. In the film's closing scene, as Batty gives up the ghost, we hear Gaff's voice, and then the man himself comes into view:

> Gaff: You've done a man's job, sir. I guess you're through, huh?
> Deckard: Finished.

He throws Deckard his gun, dropped in the fight with Batty. The figures, we see, serve as a sort of commentary. Initially at risk of being a cowardly chicken, in the end Deckard shows himself to be a man. Gaff's final remark – "It's too bad she won't live. But then again, who does?" – takes us to the film's closing scene and to the third figure he produces.

We see Deckard entering his apartment, gun in hand, anxiously calling to Rachael. It's unclear at first whether what is on his bed covered head-to-toe by a sheet is she, her corpse, or something else. As he places his cheek next to hers, she awakens:

> Deckard: Do you love me?
> Rachael: I love you.
> Deckard: Do you trust me?
> Rachael: I trust you.

No question of ventriloquism this time, it seems. With Deckard in the lead, gun still in hand, the two make their way out into the corridor. As they do, Rachael's foot knocks over a small figure made of silver foil. Deckard picks it up. The camera focuses in on it until it fills the screen.

We again hear Gaff's final words to Deckard, which now become the film's own final words: "It's too bad she won't live. But then again, who does?" As Deckard crushes the figure in his hand, he nods in assent. He accepts not just Rachael's mortality, it seems, but his own. It isn't only love that's mortal, the film seems to say, lovers – Replicant *and* human – are, too.

With the repetition of Gaff's words, death's dominion seems to have become universal, so that souls and the distinction they seem to legitimate between human and Replicant are at last abandoned. Everyone is in the same, dark boat. The unicorn figure, however, destabilizes that thought. Deckard has told Rachael that her memories are implants. As he goes to get her a drink, she runs off. When we return to the scene, after watching the one in which Pris meets Sebastian, he is sitting at the piano, his head on the keyboard, his fingers picking out a fragmentary melody. As he seems to fall into a dream, we seem to see it with him. A white unicorn charges towards us, twisting its head to gore something with its horn. When the dream evaporates, the screen fills with a close-up of Deckard's family photographs. The message, apparently, is that his dream is an implant that is known to Gaff, his photographs, fakes. Like Rachael, he is a Replicant – mortal, but also soulless.

Figure 4.1 Still from *Blade Runner* (Final Cut) Dir. Ridley Scott (2007)

Well, that is one possible message, one way to read Gaff's final figure. But there is also another. In one of his notebooks, Leonardo da Vinci gives voice to some common lore about how unicorns finally get hunted and captured: "The unicorn, through its intemperance and not knowing how to control itself, for the love it bears to fair maidens forgets its ferocity and wildness; and laying aside all fear it will go up to a seated damsel and go to sleep in her lap, and thus the hunters take it."[12] Deckard knows this lore,[13] we may suppose, and dreams about a unicorn because he has already begun to fall for Rachael, and – subliminally – to register the consequences. In the business of hunting Replicants, by coming to love one he has made himself prey to their hunters. "Would you come after me? Hunt me?" Rachael asks him after she has saved him from Leon. "No. No. I wouldn't," he replies. "I owe you one. But somebody would."

When Gaff says, "You've done a man's job, sir," he may simply be expressing in more refined – and more ironically ambiguous terms – what Bryant says more bluntly by calling Deckard "a goddamn one-man slaughterhouse." His remark about Rachael's longevity, however, suggests that he has something else in mind. It is a man's job to kill his enemies *and* to fall in love with the beautiful damsel – even if she is of enemy blood herself. By throwing him his gun, Gaff aligns himself as much with the love as with the slaughter. If he were simply Bryant's agent, he would hardly give a weapon to a man who declares himself "finished," before he has carried out all the boss's orders. "There's three to go," Deckard says when he has killed Zhora. "There's four," Bryant replies. "Now there's that skin-job you V-K'd at the Tyrell Corp. Rachael."

On this reading, Gaff makes his final silver foil figure, as he does the others, to register what Deckard has become. He is not a chicken, not a macho phallic guy, but a real man.

By offering us these two ways of understanding Gaff's unicorn, *Blade Runner* leaves us with the question of what is at stake between them. Is the issue that of whether Deckard has a soul, or whether he is capable of empathy and love? "You know that Voight-Kampff test of yours," Rachael asks him, "did you ever take that test yourself?" If Replicant love is or can become real love, however, the question of who has a soul may not matter all that much.

Notes

1 Unless otherwise identified, quotations are from the soundtrack of the final cut of the film. The opening ones are from Bryant's first conversation with Deckard.
2 A notion first introduced into philosophy by Sydney Shoemaker (1970).
3 George Eliot (1860, book II, ch. 1, final paragraph).
4 Mary Shelley (1992, vol. II, ch. 2, p. 103).
5 The Greek verb Matthew (26:47–50) and Mark (14:44–5) use to describe it is *kataphilein*, which means to kiss firmly, intensely, and passionately.
6 John Milton (1667, book IV, line 110).
7 René Descartes (1993[1641], Second Meditation, pp. 17–20).
8 The classic statement of the position is in Harry G. Frankfurt (1988).
9 A view defended by Bernard Williams (1973).
10 Friedrich Schlegel (1971, p. 241).
11 Sigmund Freud (1957, pp. 305–7).
12 Leonardo da Vinci (1998).
13 Or Ridley Scott does.

References

Da Vinci, L. (1998) *The Notebooks of Leonardo da Vinci*, Oxford: Oxford University Press.

Descartes, R. (1993[1641])*Meditations on First Philosophy*, Indianapolis: Hackett.

Eliot, G. (1860) *The Mill on the Floss*, Edinburgh: William Blackwood.

Frankfurt, H. (1988) "Freedom of the Will and the Concept of a Person" and "Alternate Possibilities and Responsibility," in *The Importance of What We Care About*, Cambridge: Cambridge University Press.

Freud, S. (1957) "On Transience," in *The Standard Edition of the Complete Psychological Works of Sigmund Freud*, London: The Hogarth Press.

Milton, J. (1667) *Paradise Lost*, London: Samuel Simmons.

Schlegel, F. (1971) *Lucinde and the Fragments*, Minneapolis: University of Minnesota Press.

Shelley, M. (1992) *Frankenstein*, London: Penguin Books.

Shoemaker, S. (1970) "Persons and their Pasts," *American Philosophical Quarterly*, 7(4): 269–85.

Williams, B. (1973) "The Self and the Future," in *Problems of the Self*, Cambridge: Cambridge University Press.

Chapter 5

Colin Allen

DO HUMANS DREAM OF EMOTIONAL MACHINES?

MUCH OF MY PROFESSIONAL LIFE has been spent thinking about the cognitive abilities of nonhuman animals. Animals are similar to us, yet simultaneously different. Across many different cultures at many different times, humans have addressed questions about who we are by comparing ourselves to the things most similar to us – both real and imagined. The real things most similar to us are other animals. The imagined categories have included angels, demiurges, and anthropomorphic gods, along with various humaniform monsters, and, more recently, space aliens. Robots, including androids, are an interesting hybrid category: once imaginary, yet increasingly a real part of our shared environment, they are particularly interesting because they may be simultaneously infrahuman, in some respects, and superhuman, in others.

Blade Runner attempts to depict "what it's like" to be a replicant. This is not mere prurient interest. A fundamental philosophical question, perhaps secondary only to "What is the meaning of life?" is "Who are we?" (Equivalently: what is distinctive about being human?) Both of these questions are raised by Scott's movie. But here I'm especially interested in the latter. It is, crucially, a comparative question.

The "imagineers" of science fiction may even play a causative role in inspiring engineers to bring imagination to reality. Thus, Douglas Engelbart, who is known as the "father of modern robotics," gives tribute to Isaac Asimov, not just for the trivial fact of Asimov's invention of the term "robotics," but for inspiring Engelbart's work in industrial robotics. It is tempting, therefore, to read or view science fiction as a form of prophecy, and with hindsight we can assess its success as such. However, it is not necessary (and perhaps not even advisable) to read science fiction as prophecy. Nevertheless, the "prophetic" reading of science fiction provides one possible answer for those who wonder how we can learn about the world, rather than merely about our concepts, from fiction. But it would be complicated to explain how that works.

To evaluate *Blade Runner* as prophecy is not the main point of this essay, however. Mainly I am concerned with the way in which the film gets us to think philosophically about what it is to be human, and, more specifically, to reflect on the role of emotions in our mental make-up. I argue that the treatment of emotion at the center of *Blade Runner* is, quite literally, ambiguous, but that this ambiguity is essential to the role of the film as springboard for philosophy. While ambiguity is essential and valuable in this role, it is a double-edged sword for prophecy. Ambiguity is, after all, the ancient parlor trick of astrologers and other foretellers of fortune. *Blade Runner* is consequently, at best, only partially successful in imagining the future applications of android robots. It gets almost nothing right about the actual technology of robot and android development as of 2015, unless its vague references to genetic engineering gain some purchase.

After the opening credits and to the accompaniment of the atmospheric score by Vangelis, words scroll up the screen, introducing the central objects of interest in the movie:

> Early in the 21st Century, the Tyrell Corporation advanced Robot evolution into the NEXUS phase – a being virtually identical to a human – known as a Replicant. The NEXUS 6 Replicants were superior in strength and agility, and at least equal in intelligence, to the genetic engineers who created them.

The replicants are described as "virtually identical," but – as the movie soon makes clear – they are not entirely identical to humans, especially with respect to typical human emotions.

The centrality of emotions to human experience is, of course, a common trope in science fiction, explored with such icons as 2001's

H.A.L., and *Star Trek*'s Mr Spock and Commander Data. These explorations have ancient roots in Stoic philosophy, which treated emotions as impediments to rational decision making. There have also been countervailing voices in Western philosophy, for instance Hume, who famously wrote, "Reason is, and ought only to be the slave of the passions, and can never pretend to any other office than to serve and obey them" (1975, Treatise Book II, part 3, section 1, p. 399). Despite Hume, the separation and opposition of cognition and emotion continued to have a strong influence on scientific and philosophical thought. Nevertheless, the idea that emotions and reason should be working in concert, not opposed, has more recently been taken up by scientists and popularized by books such as Antonio Damasio's *Descartes' Error* (1994) and Daniel Goleman's *Emotional Intelligence* (1996).

If the first four-and-a-half minutes of *Blade Runner* are essential to establishing a mood (as Amy Coplan argues in her chapter in this volume), the first scripted scene introduces the central theme of emotions as the characteristics by which the replicants may be distinguished from humans. This is the scene in which Leon, one of the four replicants who have made their way back to Earth from the other planets where they had been conscripted as slave labor, is given the "Voight-Kampff" test that is designed to detect his abnormal emotionality.

I shall have more to say about this test below. But first, a brief return to the notion that the movie gets some of its predictions right. The four fugitive replicants are first introduced to Rick Deckard in the scene where he is coerced by his former boss, Bryant, back into the job of being a "blade runner." Images on a police monitor reveal that Leon's designated function is "Combat / Loader (Nuc. Fiss.)." Roy Batty, whom Bryant describes as "Probably the leader," is shown on the monitor as "Func: Combat, Colonization Defense Prog." Bryant tells Deckard that the third replicant, Zhora, is "trained for an off-world kick-murder squad," while her police file shows "Func: Retrained (9 Feb, 2018) Polit. Homicide." Finally, Pris ("Func: Military / Leisure") is introduced by Bryant as "A basic pleasure model. The standard item for military clubs in the outer colonies."

These functions of slave labor, combat, and pleasure correspond closely to the very rapid developments in robotics that are taking place now, early in the twenty-first century. The Roomba robotic vacuum cleaner is already a commercial success, and South Korea has set a target of a robot in every home within the next couple of years. Meanwhile, iRobot Corporation, the Roomba's manufacturer and a spin-off from the Massachusetts Institute of Technology, is selling its Packbot model to the United States Army for deployment in Iraq and elsewhere. All military forces are working with various manufacturers to produce increasingly autonomous robots for logistical support, mine sweeping, and direct combat. More benignly, perhaps, the development of robots for care of the elderly is proceeding apace, and there is considerable emphasis on making such robots sociable and thus pleasurable to interact with. And if there's a way to use a technology for sexual pleasure, the history of technology teaches us that the sex industry will provide an economic engine to drive the necessary developments.

Ron Arkin, a roboticist at Georgia Tech, captures this range of applications with the phrase "Bombs, Bonding, and Bondage" – the title of a paper he wrote in 2004. This slogan neatly evokes not just the range of applications for robots that is anticipated in *Blade Runner*, and whose technological development is currently under way, but also the ethical issues they raise. By the time Deckard has been introduced to the androids by Bryant, the movie has already set up the ethical issues bidirectionally: both through the references to human treatment of replicants as expendable slaves, surrogate killers, and sex objects, and with respect to replicant treatment of humans, with the violence unleashed by Leon in his exit from the Voight-Kampff test.

Bryant continues his description of the "skin jobs" to Deckard.

> Bryant: They were designed to copy human beings in every way except their emotions. The designers reckoned that after a few years they might develop their own emotional responses. Y'know, hate, love, fear, envy.

The ambiguity of Bryant's statement is central to a number of the philosophical issues raised by the movie. Does he mean that the replicants are initially just like humans, except that they lack emotions? Or does he mean that they are just like humans except that they have different emotions? And does the development of "their own emotional responses" indicate acquisition of the human emotions – hate, love, etc. – or does it point toward *sui generis* "robotic" versions of them? The movie itself does not resolve these questions (and neither can any account of truth in fiction), which is why I side with those who think it does not constitute an *argument* for any specific view about the nature of human and nonhuman emotions. Nevertheless it provides an effective springboard for raising philosophical questions about the nature and possibility of android psychology – not just a jumping-off point, but a flexible launcher for a variety of conceptual twists that would not be so easily attained otherwise.

The ambiguous status of android emotions is instrumental in setting up a central conceit of the story:

Bryant: So they built in a fail-safe device.
Deckard: Which is what?
Bryant: Four year life span.

This limited lifespan provides only a limited time for experience and emotional development, and is a source of resentment for the replicants – an emotion that Roy Batty memorably expresses in his scene with Tyrell, his maker: "I want more life, fucker." (As the editors note in their introduction, the "Final Cut" version changes the f-word here to "father," which changes the emotional texture, but is no less emotionally resonant for the context.) Tyrell attempts to fob Batty off with some pseudoscientific mumbo-jumbo about genes and evolution that is par for the course for most science fiction. But there is irony in the fact that Tyrell's demise at Batty's hands (literally) is caused by resentment at the very fact that was supposed to provide the fail-safe device.

If the biology is mumbo-jumbo, what about the psychology? I think it is fair to say that the movie is as much Psy-Fi as it is Sci-Fi. And yet it manages to raise a number of important issues in the philosophy of mind and philosophy of cognitive science. Here are four that I touch upon below: What is the relationship of emotion to cognition? What is the nature of ethical decision making? How do developmental constraints affect mind? And to what extent does cognitive and emotional development depend on relationships to others?

I shall explore these questions through a notion of emotional checking, understood in three different ways. First, there is the sense in which the Voight-Kampff test is designed to check (i.e. verify) emotions in a one-way kind of test. Second, there is the sense in which emotions may check (i.e. restrain) actions, or motivate other actions, and the consequences of such checking on acceptable behavior. Third, there is the sense in which trusting relationships are built upon a kind of emotional checking (i.e. reciprocal, two-way give and take) that provides a foundation for cooperation built upon love, trust, and other forms of emotional bonds.

Emotional checks 1: Testing

Figure 5.1 Still from *Blade Runner* (Final Cut) Dir. Ridley Scott (2007)

Emotional checking in the first sense comes up immediately at the beginning of the movie with Leon's Voight-Kampff test. The dialogue can give only part of the picture, as anyone watching the movie can tell that Leon is emotionally distressed by the procedure, administered by the expendable character Holden:

> Holden: The tortoise lays on its back, its belly baking in the hot sun beating its legs trying to turn itself over but it can't – not without your help – but you're not helping.
>
> Leon: What do you mean I'm not helping?
>
> Holden: I mean, you're not helping. Why is that Leon?
> (pause)
>
> Holden: They're just questions, Leon. In answer to your query, they're written down for me. It's a test, designed to provoke an emotional response.
> (pause)
>
> Holden: Shall we continue? Describe in single words, only the good things that come into your mind about . . . your mother.

This question is the last Holden ever asks, as he is blasted through the wall behind him by the force of the shot fired from under the table by Leon. Whether or not Ridley Scott is intentionally suggesting a Freudian motive by having this question trigger Leon's violence, the fact that replicants lack actual mothers plays a role later in the movie too.

It is instructive to compare the Voight-Kampff test to the much-discussed Turing test of artificial intelligence. Turing's test is a purely verbal test; all non-verbal clues are eliminated from the situation, and the questioner must detect the machine by means of typed questions and answers only. In contrast, the Voight-Kampff test uses a variety of non-verbal cues. We first meet Tyrell as he speculates about what the test involves.

Tyrell: Is this to be an empathy test? Capillary dilation of the so-called blush response? Fluctuation of the pupil? Involuntary dilation of the iris?
Deckard: We call it Voight-Kampff for short.
Rachael: Mr. Deckard, Dr. Eldon Tyrell.
Tyrell: Demonstrate it. I want to see it work.
Deckard: Where's the subject?
Tyrell: I want to see it work on a person. I want to see a negative before I provide you with a positive.
Deckard: What's that going to prove?
Tyrell: Indulge me.
Deckard: On you?
Tyrell: Try her.

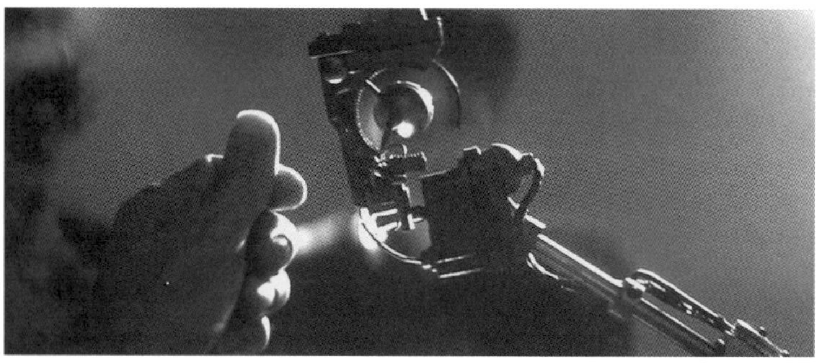

Figure 5.2 Still from *Blade Runner* (Final Cut) Dir. Ridley Scott (2007)

Deckard sets up his equipment and proceeds to question Rachael, running through a longer sequence of questions than usual.

Deckard: One more question. You're watching a stage play. A banquet is in progress. The guests are enjoying an appetizer of raw oysters. The entree consists of boiled dog.
Tyrell: Would you step out for a few moments, Rachael?
(pause)
Tyrell: Thank you.
Deckard: She's a Replicant, isn't she?
Tyrell: I'm impressed. How many questions does it usually take to spot them?

Tyrell is clearly pleased that it has taken so long for Deckard to detect that Rachael is not human, while Deckard is just as clearly disturbed by that outcome.

As a piece of fiction, this works well, but once again it fails a scientific smell test. Why, particularly in the highly Asian-ized context of Ridley Scott's Los Angeles, should it be assumed that an arbitrary individual will find the idea of eating a dog revolting? In Philip Dick's novel on which the movie is based, no such problem arises because it is one of the central ideas of *Do Androids Dream of Electric Sheep?* that because of some unspecified ecological disaster, real, live animals are exceedingly rare, very expensive, strongly protected by law, and highly desirable as pets. In *Blade Runner*, the test questions come across as culturally relative tools at best, which should also make us reflect on the diagnostic status of human emotional reactions. People from different backgrounds have widely varying reactions to suggestions of eating the family pet, or even to the emotional valence of keeping a dog in the house (a disgusting idea in some human cultures). This should make us question whether the Voight-Kampff test would reliably allow humans to be identified as such. But perhaps the test would work for a different reason. The acquisition of such cultural norms is a lengthy process in human development. Given the necessity for extensive cultural experience in establishing normatively specific reactions in people, it is implausible that a creature with merely a four-year lifespan could build up the store of experiences needed to have "normal" reactions to such things. Here the movie takes a new tack: could the bases for human-like emotions be implanted?

In Dick's novel, Rachael is coldly trying to force Deckard to give away the secrets of the test. But in *Blade Runner*, she is an unwitting guinea-pig:

Tyrell: Commerce, is our goal here at Tyrell. More human than human is our motto. Rachael is an experiment, nothing more. We began to recognize in them strange obsessions. After all they are emotionally inexperienced with only a few years in which to store up the experiences which you and I take for granted. If we give them the past we create a cushion or pillow for their emotions and consequently we can control them better.

Deckard: Memories. You're talking about memories.

Memory is a recurring theme in *Blade Runner* and a key prop is the use of photographs to support them. Rachael comes to Deckard's apartment clutching a photograph purportedly of her mother and herself as a young girl. Deckard's own apartment contains a collection of old photographs that help fuel the controversy among moviegoers and critics over whether he is himself a replicant. This kind of externalization of autobiographical memory in the souvenirs of a life is perhaps what primarily drives us to clutter our shelves with items that, for the most part, become other people's junk. These items trigger a kind of emotional specificity that is harder to achieve without them. Just as chance encounters with a smell of a certain food or perfume can trigger richly emotional memories of the past – home cooking, an absent lover – so too can the rediscovery of a photograph or a toy or a trophy bring back not just names and places, but feelings that provide autobiographical authenticity. We also remember things without external props, particularly those with strong emotional valence.

During Rachael's visit to his apartment, Deckard reveals that he knows details of her purported life for which there are no external mementos:

Deckard: Yeah. (pause) Remember when you were six? You and your brother snuck into an empty building through a basement window – you were gonna play doctor. He showed you his, but when it got to be your turn you chickened out and ran. Remember that? You ever tell anybody that? Your mother, Tyrell, anybody? You remember the spider that lived in a bush outside your window: orange body, green legs. Watched her build a web all summer. Then one day there was a big egg in it. The egg hatched –

Rachael: The egg hatched, and a hundred baby spiders came out. And they ate her.

Deckard: Implants! Those aren't your memories. They're somebody else's. They're Tyrell's niece's.

Rachael is devastated. Deckard attempts to backpedal by claiming it is a joke. But the movie script succeeds by introducing the kind of memories that the viewers intuitively grasp as having strong emotional content: a first sexual experience, watching a mother being eaten by her own offspring. Regardless of the plausibility of a Voight-Kampff test which tests emotional responses externally, there's another sense of emotional check which is internal – the felt difference between remembering something one did and remembering something one merely has heard about.

Emotional checks 2: Restraining

In describing Rachael to Deckard as an experiment, Tyrell invokes the metaphor of the created past as a cushion or pillow for the replicants' emotions. Exactly how this metaphor applies is vague – providing comfort, softening a blow? – and perhaps deliberately so. Regardless, the relationship between cognitive aspects of autobiographical memory (who, what, when, where?) and emotion is more complex than the metaphor suggests. Pillows conform to what presses upon them, but emotions and memories shape each other. The "how I felt" aspect of a memory is perhaps the only component of an original experience that can be literally recreated. By exploiting the interplay between external cues and powerful feelings *Blade Runner* correctly imagines the role of emotional checks in human experience.

Roy Batty's final soliloquy in the pouring rain is justly one of the most celebrated scenes in the movie. Having already killed Tyrell, Roy saves Deckard's life after almost killing him too. His own life is coming to an end due to the programmed obsolescence.

Figure 5.3 Still from *Blade Runner* (Final Cut) Dir. Ridley Scott (2007)

> Roy: I've seen things you people wouldn't believe. Attack ships on fire off the shoulder of Orion. I watched sea beams glitter in the darkness at Tannhäuser Gate. All those moments will be lost in time like tears in rain. Time to die.

Here, then, memory does indeed serve as a kind of emotional cushion. Roy has seen things. For himself. Things he believes his creators are incapable of fully grasping. The authenticity of those memories and his satisfaction in their authenticity makes it okay not to kill Deckard. Anger is buffered by his own satisfaction with his own experienced life, no matter how short. It turns out for Roy that curtailing the lives of others is less important than having been the author of one's own life. And one might speculate that he realizes that if he kills Deckard now, not only will those moments in other worlds be lost in time, but this one will too.

To this point, the movie has emphasized far more the negative emotions than the positive emotions . . .

> Bryant: Y'know, hate, love, fear, envy.

. . . a three to one ratio. In this respect scientific psychology is not very different. Paul Ekman's seminal work on the basic emotions listed anger, disgust, fear, happiness, sadness, and surprise, and even though the list has since been expanded, research on emotions still tends to focus on negative emotions such as fear and anger. There are clinical and societal reasons for this focus: negative emotions would seem to lead to harm much more often than positive emotions, so there are good reasons for trying to understand and regulate them. But positive emotions may be part of the regulatory mix; satisfaction in one's own life can indeed modulate anger.

But wouldn't things be better without anger at all? If there's no anger to check, then there's no need to worry about anger leading to bad consequences. Wouldn't a machine that neither hated nor loved be more manageable than one that "has its own emotions," to quote Bryant again. The Stoic presupposition against the emotions is apparent among some current roboticists. Here is Ron Arkin, on the prospects for autonomous battlefield robots: "They can be designed without emotions that cloud their judgment or result in anger and frustration with ongoing battlefield events. In addition, 'Fear and hysteria are always latent in combat, often real, and they press us toward fearful measures and criminal behavior' [quoting Walzer 1977, p. 251]. Autonomous agents need not suffer similarly."

But while the Stoic view of rationality and ethics sees emotions as irrelevant and dangerous to making ethically correct decisions, the more recent literature on emotional intelligence suggests that emotional input is essential to rational and ethical behavior. In his work on governing lethal behavior in battlefield robots, Arkin has made a slight concession, allowing that some attempt to model the "moral emotions" may be important. He lists the moral emotions from Jonathan Haidt's taxonomy: contempt, anger, disgust, shame, embarrassment, guilt, compassion, gratitude, elevation. (Again, the predominance of negative emotions is apparent.) Arkin writes that "an architectural component modeling a subset of these affective components (initially only guilt) is intended to serve as an adaptive learning function for the autonomous system architecture should it act in error."

Of course, even apparently negative emotions such as anger may be righteous, providing important motivation for righting injustices, etc. But the picture so far is one of individual emotions being experienced from the inside or "read" from the outside. This picture is incomplete. Whether it is the positive or negative emotions that are being considered as drivers and inhibitors of human (or human-like) behavior, there is a further, social aspect of emotional checking, which *Blade Runner* explores after the departure of Roy Batty.

Emotional checks 3: Reciprocating

Deckard: Do you love me?
Rachael: I love you.
Deckard: Do you trust me?
Rachael: I trust you.

Love and trust are functional when they are reciprocated. Does Deckard's willingness to commit himself to a replicant stem from the reprieve he gets from Roy? The movie makes no essential claims about what is required for love and trust between Deckard and Rachael. It merely shows their relationship. And, notoriously, the original theatrical release and the director's cut versions leave the outcome of that relationship ambiguous to different degrees. We should not expect clear thesis statements from movies. Nevertheless, by raising the issues of trust and love in a context where there is ambiguity about the very nature of the emotions belonging to the two parties, the movie opens up a philosophical discussion of the ethics and psychology of trust in humans.

In a recent, non-fictional case, a US serviceman serving in Iraq wrote to iRobot Corporation, begging them to repair his PackBot that had been blown to pieces by an improvised explosive device. "Please fix Scooby Doo. He saved my life," he wrote. The serviceman did not want a new PackBot, he wanted that very one made whole again. Their relationship had been forged over multiple missions, and despite (or perhaps because of) the utterly mechanical nature of Scooby Doo, the level of trust was very high. With trust comes loyalty and love. If the soldier's loyalty to Scooby Doo is dysfunctional, it is because the relationship is one-way. Outside the operational context of the war zone there would be little to sustain it.

But trust is normally individualized and contextualized. I may trust you with my finances but not my car, or vice versa. One may have a bias toward trusting strangers, or against, but neither is a sufficient basis for rational decision making and ethical engagement with others. What's needed is trust of *this* individual, gained through a series of increasingly committed interactions. *Blade Runner* depicts a strong bond among the replicants themselves, built upon their shared experiences. The growing trust between Deckard and Rachael is also built upon experience. In the end, *Blade Runner*'s treatment of the emotional development of the replicants themselves and of Deckard (whether human or not) is far more interesting and compelling as science fiction than the more overt and blithe assumption that autobiographical memories can be crafted by technologists to be plugged in at will. Cognitive science has recently woken up to the idea that who we are and what we are capable of depends as much on resources external to ourselves as it does on those to be found in the brain alone. In this regard, *Blade Runner* is equivocal, but it was not intended to be a coherent piece of philosophy. Much has been written about the physical messiness of Ridley Scott's vision of the future Los Angeles. The movie's emotional messiness, however, is just as significant and perhaps even more likely to be prophetic of the profound effects on ourselves that will follow from the development of machines that seem, at least, to care.

References

Arkin, R. (2004) "Bombs, Bonding, and Bondage: Human-Robot Interaction and Related Ethical Issues," unpublished paper presented at the First International Symposium on Roboethics, San Remo, Italy.

Damasio, A. (1994) *Descartes' Error: Emotion, Reason, and the Human Brain*, New York: Putnam.

Goleman, D. (1996) *Emotional Intelligence*, New York: Bantam House.

Hume, D. (1975) *A Treatise of Human Nature*, ed. L. A. Selby-Bigge, rev. P. H. Nidditch, Oxford: Clarendon Press.

Walzer, M. (1977) *Just and Unjust Wars*, New York: Basic Books.

Chapter 6

Stephen Mulhall

ZHORA THROUGH THE LOOKING-GLASS

NOTES ON AN ESPER ANALYSIS OF LEON'S PHOTOGRAPH

> One of the more interesting concepts in Hampton's and People's scripts was the Esper. That was supposed to be this talking supercomputer run by the police. Originally, it was going to be everywhere – inside cars, out on the sidewalk, everywhere. But that got whittled away during rewrites until the Esper only made two appearances. One was as the small terminal in Deckard's apartment through which he runs Leon's photograph. The other was in the Blue Room [at Police Headquarters]: we called the monitors screening the replicants' Incept Tapes the 'Esper Wall'.
>
> Terry Rawlings (editor, *Blade Runner*)

> Harrison [Ford] examining that photograph is one of my favourite sequences in the film, because it says 'Watch me create a lie' . . . [T]he photo itself is a lie – you think only one person's in that room, but there are two.
>
> So that whole Esper sequence shows how you can play with images and tell a story, and at the same time, completely bullshit someone. Which is just like making a motion picture, come to think of it. But the truth of that photo is – there is no truth.
>
> Rutger Hauer ('Roy Batty')[1]

1) Deckard finds the photograph amongst a sheaf of others, tucked beneath a stack of towels bundled into a drawer in Leon's room at the Yukon Hotel, 1187 Hunterwasser Street – abandoned after Leon's murderous attack on Deckard's ex-colleague Holden. Ridley Scott places

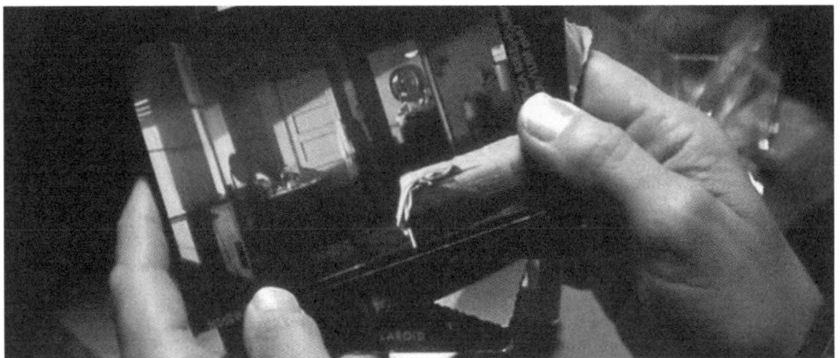

Figure 6.1 Still from *Blade Runner* (Final Cut) Dir. Ridley Scott (2007)

Deckard's sudden attraction to this particular image between two views of its creator: before the discovery, we see Leon on the street outside, halted in his progress towards the hotel by the sight of a light in that room; after it, we see him admit to his fellow-replicant that he was too late to rescue what Roy sneeringly calls his 'precious photographs' – too late to recover these prosthetic memories of his replicant family.

The photograph that draws Deckard's eye is strikingly, mysteriously beautiful, and so leaps out from its seedy surroundings, even though it is, in effect, an image of them. For the space it depicts is that of a cheap hotel room – very probably the one in which it is discovered; but the manner of its depiction is reminiscent not only of many such rooms in Edward Hopper's paintings, but also (even more strongly) of the Dutch interiors of Vermeer. Such nostalgic prescience, the imagined American future as a restaging of the mid-twentieth century as seen by seventeenth-century Europe (which itself echoes the film's presentation of a blade runner as Philip Marlowe *redivivus*, in a twenty-first century Los Angeles as envisioned by a twentieth-century Englishman making his first foray into Hollywood), is conjured partly by the photograph's formal features – the sturdily balanced way in which the various objects in the room are placed in relation to its walls, its windows, and to the viewer – and partly by the way this arrangement of objects is illuminated.

The middle ground of the photograph consists of one long wall, running parallel to the picture plane, in the precise centre of which appear two rectangles of identical shape and size, like the panels of a diptych or the leaves of an open book. To the immediate left of centre, there is a closed door with a towel or item of clothing suspended from its handle;

immediately to the right of centre, there is an open doorway leading into a second room, within which we can dimly see a bureau above which hangs a circular mirror in an elaborate frame. To the left of the closed door, and a little further into the first room, is a table with various objects and papers scattered on its surface; beyond it, and set flush against the short left-hand wall of the room, is a chest-of-drawers with the ellipsoid outline of a circular mirror sitting on top. To the right of the open doorway, we can see (low against the wall) what looks like a boiler next to a sink unit and mirror, then (nearer to us) a lamp on a bedside table and (in the very near foreground, presumably flush to the unseen, short right-hand wall of the room) the lower half of a made-up bed, with another towel or piece of clothing draped over its edge. Table, bed, chest-of-drawers, sink and bedside table are each approximately parallelepipedal, and so placed that each stands parallel to the central wall, jutting into the rectangular room at differing but collectively harmonious depths and heights (a pattern into which the bureau in the second room, set flush against its rear wall and so jutting into its correspondingly rectangular space, perfectly fits), and so parallel to the photographer, who was evidently standing with his back against the other (unseen) long wall of the first room (standing, we feel, where we now stand). This array of planes and solids – each piece locking into every other, like the mutually supporting elements of a geometrical proof – immediately seems impossible to imagine otherwise; in suggesting a necessity underlying the contingencies of the real, it presents itself as the setting for something timeless, at once eternal and dead, beyond alteration and beyond recovery. Leon may have lost the photograph (and he will come to confront the loss of the people in it), but no one can take what it represents away from him.

The scene is illuminated by sunlight shining through a pair of windows in the left-hand wall of the first room. It is cast at a shallow upward angle (so the sun must be low, and the room most likely high in the hotel), and it has a pale but intense quality that suggests afternoon rather than morning. It reaches across the whole space, and gives a quietly magical richness and depth to the various everyday things it touches, conveying the volume of space that each occupies, capturing the substantial transparencies of glass and reflection, and distinguishing clearly between subtly varying shades of cream, very light green and brown. But this light also casts strong shadows, so we do not immediately realize that, at the table on the left near the window, we can see the shoulder and arm of a man whose head is turned away from us and is anyway (along with the rest of his body) in starkly contrastive darkness – someone as still and substantial as any of the objects surrounding him: just one more solidly material, quotidian thing on which the setting sun casts its indifferently transfigurative light.

Can a Hollywood science fiction movie really claim to take the measure of, and so to measure itself against, the kind of artistic ambition exemplified by Vermeer? At the very least, the sheer presence and the unfolding purpose of this photographic mimesis of ordinary life suggests an interest on Scott's part in reflecting on the relative powers and constraints of painting and photography, and thereby on the material basis of his own cinematographic medium.

2) Deckard's Esper analysis of the photograph is preceded by two other contextualizations of it – two other sets of associations established between it and other sheaves of photographs. The first such sheaf belongs to Rachael, the new-generation Nexus replicant identified as such by Deckard at the Tyrell Corporation. Until that Voight-Kampff interrogation, Rachael had been ignorant of her own nature, since she had been given (as a pillow or cushion for her emotions) a set of memory implants derived from Tyrell's niece. Hence, when she confronts Deckard in his apartment after his return from the Yukon Hotel, she tries to establish her human status by presenting him with one of her family photographs – in particular, with a snapshot of herself as a child with her mother; and Deckard rebuts her attempt by describing to her a couple of childhood memories so private or trivial that she could not have recounted them to anyone else (all part of the set of implants to which Rachael's photograph must correspond). Seeing her distress, he tries half-heartedly to withdraw his remarks, but is relieved to see her take the first opportunity to depart. However, she leaves behind the photograph she brought, and when Deckard discovers it, he undergoes an uncanny experience that we share with him.

For a brief moment, we see the shadows in the photograph ripple and sway, and hear the sound of children shouting and laughing; in other words, this still photograph acquires movement and a voice – it becomes a miniaturized motion picture with synchronized soundtrack, as if not so much representing as fusing with or becoming part of the very medium which presents it to us.[2] Deckard experiences a photograph of the past as if that past were really present to him, as if it were not only what really happened (for how else could Tyrell have had anything to implant in Rachael's memory?) but really as much his – alive to him, his to own – as Rachael's; and yet his hallucinated identification with Rachael simply confirms his powerlessness with respect to that reality, since Rachael herself must learn to disown it (to acknowledge it as owned by another). And in experiencing with Deckard this impotent apprehension of reality, we find ourselves confronting a movie within the movie we are watching. So are we being told that a motion picture presents us with nothing less than reality (as opposed to a mere representation or likeness of it), or nothing more than a world from which I am absent? Both.

> The reality in a photograph is present to me while I am not present to it; and a world I know, and see, but to which I am nevertheless not present (through no fault of my own) is a world past. In viewing a movie . . . I am present not at something happening, which I must confirm, but at something that has happened, which I must absorb (like a memory).
>
> (Stanley Cavell 1971, pp. 23, 25–6)

In theatre, although we cannot occupy the same space as the characters in a play (since there is no path that can be traversed from our location to theirs), we can occupy the same time (by confronting with them the present moment of the play's events without importing either our knowledge of its ending or any assumption that what has already happened must dictate their fate). But as viewers of a photograph or a film, we share neither a space nor a time with the object or person photographed; we are not in its physical presence, and the moment at which the object was captured by the camera cannot be made present by us (for our absence is mechanically, automatically assured). My claim is that Ridley Scott knows this, and invites us to see it, here and now, in this movie.

3) Deckard's uncanny apprehension of Rachael's photograph prompts him to return to his sheaf of Leon's photographs, and in particular to the one after Vermeer; but this time it emerges from the sheaf only after

he (and we) glimpse two other photographs, the first of which focuses tightly on the shoulder and arm of the man at the table, and the second of which includes rather more of the room in which he is located. The eventual re-appearance of the Vermeer photograph, which presents us once again with this man in the whole context of the room, is thereby framed as the conclusion of a flickering series. Within the world of the film, we can take this as an indication that this apparently isolated image is in fact the end-point of a sequence of discrete exposures that reflect the gradual enlargement of Leon's (and so his camera's) field of attention; but we can also understand it reflexively, as the final frame in a representative sequence of such frames abstracted from a continuous strip of film exposed by a gradually withdrawing motion picture camera. By juxtaposing the Vermeer image's recurrence to these other images of Leon's, and juxtaposing them all in turn with Rachael's photograph, Scott asks us to look backwards and forwards at once. The Vermeer photograph now carries with it an implicit declaration of its status as condition of possibility for the moving picture in which it appears; and it anticipates the process of Esper analysis to which it will soon be subjected.

4) Soon; but not quite yet. For Deckard's transition to the Esper is interrupted – partly in ways for which he is responsible, but also in ways that are the responsibility of the director of this film. Ridley Scott chooses to separate the re-appearance of the Vermeer photograph from its analysis, and so to interrupt the film's narrative of the search for the replicants, by inserting a critical sequence in the film's parallel narrative of the replicants' attempts to track down, and make direct contact with, their Maker: Tyrell. In this inserted sequence, Pris lies in wait for J. F. Sebastian outside the Bradbury Building, and persuades him to let her stay in his apartment for a while; only after she has met some of his animatroid toys, and he offers to take her bag and soaked coat, does Scott return us to Deckard's apartment. Time has passed since we left him; and as the camera tracks across from his apartment window into its dimmer depths, we are shown that Deckard has made use of that time to drink, to settle himself at his piano, and to place Leon's photograph among a raggedly assembled group of Deckard's own family photographs, now displayed along the front and top of the piano. The tracking shot ends by showing Deckard's finger on one of the piano keys: and as we see him depress the key in perfect synchronization with the playing

of a single note in the musical sequence that has accompanied the tracking shot from its beginning, we realize with a shock that Deckard has been helping to make the music we have been hearing. Once again, the supposedly clear distinction between representation and what is represented, between the film we are viewing and the world with which it presents us, has been deliberately subverted. And by engineering this particular subversion at this precise moment, Scott implies that there might be an internal relation between his editorial delaying tactics and Deckard's own deferral of action.

Clearly, by making the connection between the significance of Rachael's and Leon's photographs to them, and the significance of his own photographs to him, Deckard has begun to acknowledge that the differences between humans and replicants are less decisive or absolute than he might previously have assumed. Rather than focus on what the photographs are photographs of, he has allowed himself to focus instead on the relation between the photographs and their owners; and he has thereby begun to imagine the replicants' lives as ones in which objects can show up as meaningful, and so to imagine the replicants as beings whose lives have meaning for them – as having a life to live, to own or disown. And the inserted sequence precisely confirms this perception for us, insofar as it records the next step in their project to (as they understand it) recover their authority over their own existence, to reclaim their autonomy.

(It is therefore no accident that, when – in both the Director's Cut and the Final Cut versions of the film – Scott wishes to develop further a suggestion of Deckard's kinship with replicant modes of being, he chooses this reverie before the photographs on the piano as the moment at which to insert the notorious unicorn sequence. This brief dissolve to a mythical animal racing in slow motion out of the film's only green landscape evidently captures an evanescent moment of Deckard's inner life, and so exactly the kind of supposedly private interior event whose recollection Rachael has just erroneously relied upon to ground her sense of her own humanity. So when, in the film's final scene, we see that Gaff has left an origami unicorn outside Deckard's apartment – thereby signalling his tacit approval of Deckard's decision to shelter, and then to depart with, Rachael – we are also invited to consider the question of how Gaff could know of Deckard's vision, if not by exactly the means Deckard employed in penetrating Rachael's reserves of privacy.)

But precisely because the replicants are autonomous actors, Deckard's own decision to defer his analysis of the representational content of Leon's photograph has consequences. The time he has spent getting contemplatively drunk at the piano, allowing himself to be dreamily distracted by the seductive sequence of photographs arranged on it, is time that the replicants have employed to further their hunt for Tyrell. If Deckard had immediately begun to analyse Leon's photograph, and thereby to further his own hunt for the replicants, he might have made progress sufficiently swiftly to prevent at least some of the deaths that Roy Batty goes on to inflict. Instead, he has ensured that he will catch up with Pris in the Bradbury Building just in time to kill her, to be caught in the act by the returning Roy, and then to be turned loose in the otherwise empty building to become the subject of Roy's vengeful, and painfully corporeal, lesson in existential metaphysics. So what Scott allows us to see, in the gap between Deckard's initial realization of what he must do next and his final enactment of that necessity, is in fact the geographical setting to which he is now fated to arrive, the unavoidable, dilapidated scene of his climactic confrontation with his own mortality. In short, we see Deckard's future, during the very moments at which (by his own inaction) he is bringing it about.

5) After resurfacing from his unicorn vision, Deckard plucks out Leon's photograph from the sheaf of his own family photographs, and – his hands fully occupied with whiskey bottle and glass – carries it carefully between his teeth (like a hunting dog transferring its master's prey) to the living room area, where he inserts it into the Esper machine and settles back on the sofa.

The Esper displays a (slightly cropped) version of the photograph on its video monitor, and then – responding to a sequence of voiced commands from Deckard – proceeds to isolate and enlarge a variety of specific portions of the image (identified by Deckard in terms of a co-ordinate system superimposed by the monitor). Each enlargement process is accompanied by a sequence of clicks, exactly like the shutter on a camera; and Deckard repeatedly directs the Esper as if he were directing the movements of a motion picture camera ('Pull out, track right – stop'; 'Centre in, pull back'; 'Pan right and pull back'; 'Track 45 right'). First, he focuses on the man with his arm resting on the table to the left, and enhances the image to the point at which he (and we) can recognize

Figure 6.2 Still from *Blade Runner* (Final Cut) Dir. Ridley Scott (2007)

Roy Batty; then the Esper pans across to examine the papers on the table, which turn out to hold no particular interest. Then, as we pan further across the first room, we cross the open doorway, and Deckard spots the mirror and bureau set against the rear wall of the second room. He immediately refocuses the Esper on them – first on the various objects on the top of the bureau (desk lamp, glass, electric fan), then on the reflection dimly visible in the slightly convex mirror.

By enhancing a portion of the south-east quadrant of the mirror surface, he produces an image of an otherwise-invisible corner of the second room (the front right-hand corner, viewed from our original position in the first room); and in that corner, there is a wardrobe, with two mirrored doors slightly ajar, and something inside visible in the gap between them. Deckard commands the Esper to enhance that portion of the reflected image, and the machine very quickly enlarges it to the point at which it begins to lose its resolution. What then fills the monitor (and so our screen) is a thick vertical column of glittering ovals, overlapping with one another – a haze of yellow-white reflective surfaces: sequins, perhaps decorating a scarf or more likely a dress. Deckard pauses for a long moment; then he asks the Esper first to pull back, then – quickly – to go right, where (apparently reflected in one of the mirrored doors of the wardrobe) he sees an image of the crook of an elbow with a silver bracelet above the joint. He asks the machine to track left, panning once more across the braid of sequins to reveal (apparently reflected in the other mirrored wardrobe door) a larger image of the owner of the elbow: further tracking reveals that it belongs to a woman asleep on a divan (presumably tucked away in the opposite corner – the rear right-hand corner – of the second room to that occupied by the wardrobe, or perhaps in an alcove leading off from it), wearing a headscarf, and partly covered by a patterned black-and-white blanket. Deckard asks the Esper to focus on and enlarge the image of her face, so that he and we can see more clearly a tattoo on the hinge of her jaw – possibly an abstract symbol, more likely a snake.

Deckard says: 'Give me a hard copy right there'; the Esper disgorges a print of the woman's head in close-up, tattoo and all; and after examining it for a few seconds, Deckard retrieves and looks closely at a transparent evidence bag in which he had deposited an item he found in the bathtub of Leon's hotel room – a small, translucent oval flake. Then Scott cuts to an establishing shot of Animoid Row – the market within which Deckard will begin to search for the maker of what he now realizes is a scale from an artificial animal.

6) Why is this short sequence in *Blade Runner* at all? To begin with, what narrative purpose does it serve? On the face of it, the analysis gives Deckard a way of finding Zhora, and thereby the other replicants. Once the scale from the bathtub is examined in Animoid Row, it is revealed to be from a snake manufactured by a very superior craftsman, who directs Deckard to the nightclub owner who purchased it, and so to the exotic dancer for whom he bought it: Miss Salome, aka Zhora. But in truth, it is not at all clear exactly how the Esper's revelation of a sleeping Zhora in the otherwise invisible recesses of Leon's photograph gives Deckard any information or opportunity he didn't already possess. After all, he knows from the outset that Zhora is one of the missing band of replicants, and he knows what she looks like from the Incept Tapes Captain Bryant has earlier shown him at Police Headquarters; it is certainly hard to believe that her tattoo will provide clinching evidence of identity in a way that her face will not. One might think that the tattoo rather gives Deckard reason to consider that his evidence bag contains a snake scale – except that when he first presents it for analysis in Animoid Row, he suggests that it is a fish scale, and has to be corrected by the analyst. Is it, then, that the sequinned dress he sees between the wardrobe doors first suggests to him the idea that what he has found is a scale – whether because each glittering oval has the shape of a scale, or because the dress as a whole evokes the idea of a scaled creature? Perhaps so: but then, once again, the fact that the Esper analysis goes on to reveal

Zhora herself in Leon's set of rooms becomes entirely irrelevant to Deckard's investigative thought processes.

So it is hard to accept that the sequence's contribution to the film's plot is what justifies its presence. If, then, its inclusion is not entirely superfluous – and I am surely not alone in thinking that it is one of the most striking and absorbing sequences in the film as a whole – its reason for being must be sought elsewhere.

7) The key phenomenological fact about watching the sequence is that what we know to be a computer-aided analysis of a photograph of a room is experienced quite as if we are moving around within the room itself, able to examine any portion of it – even those out of sight from certain positions within it – and in endlessly recessive detail (every discovered grain itself containing a world). What the panning, tracking and shifts of focus effected by the Esper thereby bring out is the fact that, in viewing a photograph of three-dimensional objects in a three-dimensional space, we see nothing less or other than those very three-dimensional objects in their genuinely three-dimensional space. To put matters another way: the sequence projects the truth of Stanley Cavell's observation (1971, pp. 16–26) that the objects in a photograph do not differ in some specifiable respect from real objects, as if the former either lack or possess some feature that the latter either possess or lack. We can distinguish real objects from one another by specifying criteria, determining specific differences between (say) a goldfinch and a sparrow; and we can distinguish between the same objects in a photograph using the same criteria. But we cannot distinguish real objects from objects in a photograph in such a way; there are no criteria which distinguish a photographed object from the object itself – no specific respect (such as eye colour, height, or running style) in which Rutger Hauer in a photograph differs from Rutger Hauer in the flesh.

This does not mean that there is no difference between Rutger Hauer in a photograph and Rutger Hauer in the flesh; what it does mean is that it is not obvious how to specify that difference, and in particular that it is just wrong to attempt to specify it in certain tempting ways. If, for example, we felt tempted to say, 'But an object or person in a photograph isn't really there, right in front of our eyes', then we would either be asserting something that no-one in their right mind would deny (namely that a photograph of Rutger Hauer is not Rutger Hauer), or something flatly false (namely, that this is not a photograph of the real, the one and only, Rutger Hauer), or something empty (for existence, as Kant emphasized, is not a predicate, and so not a property or attribute predicable of the real Rutger Hauer but not predicable of Rutger Hauer in a photograph). Similarly, we cannot say that a photograph of an object is a visual representation of it (in the way that a painting of it might be); for that would suggest that it stands, or goes proxy, for it, or forms a likeness of it, whereas a photograph of Rutger Hauer does not display a likeness of him, but rather the man himself. Nor does a photograph of an object transcribe its sight or look or appearance in just the way that a sound recording can transcribe its sound. For although objects can be said to have or make sounds, they cannot be said to make or to have sights or looks or appearances; what we see when we see something in a photograph is not the look or the appearance of an object but (nothing less or other than) the object itself. In short, what the Esper sequence drives home to us is i) that there is nothing of the right sort for a photograph to be a photograph *of* short of the object itself; and ii) that we don't properly comprehend the significance of this.

8) But what is under examination in this sequence is not simply the work of the camera, but more specifically that of the motion picture camera. Leon may have produced the original image by photographic means, but our voyage within the three-dimensional space it presents to us is guided by the familiar, commanding turns of phrase addressed by a film director to his cameraman, and as the Esper takes us further into the hidden corners of that space so Deckard becomes at once more alert to, and more completely absorbed by, the reality it presents – just like the viewers of the film of which that sequence forms a part. Consequently, the truths it reveals about photography appear as truths about the material basis of the cinematic medium.[3] And if we examine more closely the key revelatory passage of the Esper analysis, we will find that it acknowledges both the undeniable reality of the world of the hotel room, and the incomprehensibility of the fact that it can be made present to us in this way, in its absence.

That passage of the analysis which takes us from the mirror in the second room, via the reflection it contains of one hidden corner of that

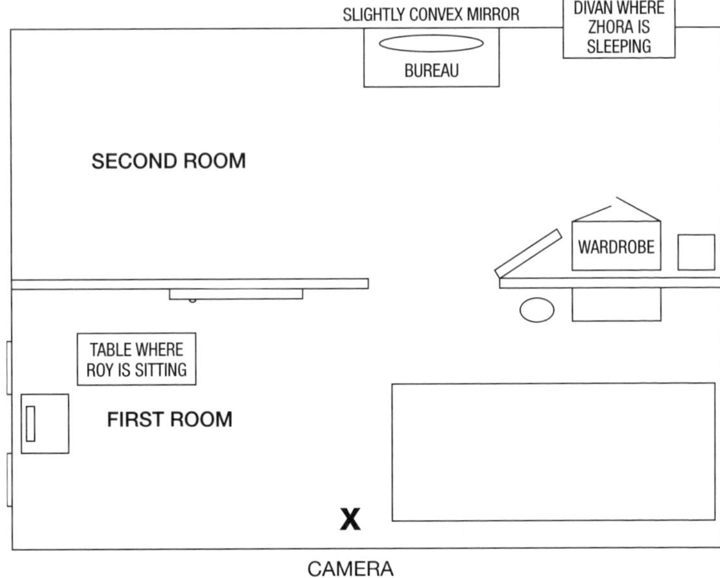

Figure 6.3 Diagram of the room in Leon's photograph. Stephen Mulhall

room, to the sequinned dress hanging in the wardrobe standing in that corner is deeply respectful of the laws of physics and geometry. The slight convexity of the mirror renders plausible the assumption that illuminated objects tucked away in the front right-hand corner of that second room would be reflected from the mirror surface at just the right angle to be captured by the eye of the camera at its implied location in the first room. The Esper's recovery of a detailed reflection of the contents of that hidden corner therefore makes perfect sense, taken as the result of analysing Leon's photograph. It thereby reinforces the reality of the room in that photograph, including the reality of the photographer's position within it (their subjection to physical law), and so the intelligibility of the photograph's very existence. One could also say that it underlines the difference between a photograph of the room and a painting of it (since the Esper analysis presupposes that it always, necessarily, makes sense to ask of a room in a photograph whether a space hidden from view within it is in fact occupied by anything or anyone, whereas this only ever makes sense accidentally when asked of a room in a painting[4]).

But in addition, it underlines the intelligibility of its being in Deckard's possession – the fact that the photograph is of a real place and real people with a real location co-ordinatable with that of his own, and so that the viewer, the maker and the subjects of this photograph inhabit a common world: one in which they might confront, or avoid or simply fail to come across, one another, but in which they cannot avoid taking responsibility for the specific position and relations they adopt within it. One might say, then, that this phase of the Esper analysis makes manifest the internal spatio-temporal coherence of the world of the film, and so our absence from it (the absence of any route from our space and time to its space and time). Nothing in the world of the film is beyond our sight; but no-one in that world is within our grasp.

The second phase of the analysis – beginning when the Esper pulls back from the sequinned dress and ending with the revelation of a sleeping woman – works very differently, however. For Deckard is now analysing a second level of reflection (those visible in the mirrored doors of the wardrobe, which are themselves reflected in the circular mirror); and the problem is that this set of reflections does not seem to obey the laws of physics and geometry. If there really were a wardrobe in that hidden front right-hand corner, standing roughly opposite to the sleeping Zhora, and with its doors opening out into the room, then the mirrored panel on its right-hand door[5] could conceivably provide a reflection of Zhora that the circular mirror might itself reflect to anyone in the position of the photograph taker. But the left-hand door could not possibly do so: if it were open, it would face towards the nearby wall of the room and so away from the circular mirror; and even if it were shut, any reflection of it in the circular mirror that was perceivable from the photographer's position, and so capturable in his photograph, could not possibly contain a reflection of someone directly opposite the wardrobe (it could only be a reflection of the nearby wall). Yet the Esper analysis seems to involve recovering partial reflections of Zhora from *both* doors (as reflected in the circular mirror); and what is more, it seems capable of altering the content of the reflection it recovers from one of those doors – by shifting focus in such a way as to bring more of the sleeping Zhora into view. But this is not the kind of new visual information that a still photograph, however intensively analysed, could possibly provide; for it could not result from enlarging an image (or any portion of an image) taken from one fixed point. It could only be done by someone who was actually in that second room, and so able to exploit the full reflective potential of those mirrored doors by altering his position with respect to them.

In other words, the point at which Deckard shifts from exploring the reflection of the wardrobe in the circular mirror to exploring the reflection in that wardrobe's mirrored doors – call it his step through the looking-glass in the looking-glass – is the point at which the sequence loses its coherence, taken as an Esper analysis of Leon's original photograph. Right up to the moment at which Deckard sees that the doors of the wardrobe are mirrored, and so might reveal portions of the second room that are still outside his field of vision, everything he has discovered from analyzing the photograph could conceivably be discoverable from it (that is: from the visual information it must contain, given the position of the one taking the photograph). But from the moment he begins to explore the reflections in those wardrobe doors, what they reveal could not conceivably be discoverable from the photograph of the room under analysis (given the fixed positions of Zhora, the doors, and the circular mirror relative to the taker and so the viewer of that photograph); it could only be discovered from the room *in* the photograph.

9) Why this sudden loss of coherence, between the first level of reflections (those in the circular mirror) and the second (those in the wardrobe doors)? If we think of that transition as registering a shift in viewpoint – from that of a viewer of the photograph to that of an inhabitant of the room photographed – then a variety of possible answers emerge. At the level of the narrative in which Deckard and the replicants are characters, this shift signals the extent to which Deckard's abilities as a blade runner are both dependent on and threatened by his capacity to empathize with his prey; he would not have uncovered everything there to be revealed in the photograph without taking on the perspective of one of the room's inhabitants (i.e. one of the replicant family), but it is precisely his willingness to acknowledge the replicants as his others – as occupying the kind of perspective on existence that he occupies – that will lead him to join Rachael on the other side of the law. The uncanny, incomprehensible transition between these two phases of his photographic analysis is thus an indication of a developing fissure in his own identity, a growing sense of himself as fatally obscure to himself, as if something essential to who and what he is stands beyond his own grasp.

At the level of the film's broader themes, this shift of viewpoint implicates the viewers of *Blade Runner* in Deckard's growing appreciation of the replicants as really possessed of a humanly inhabitable, perhaps even a genuinely human, point of view. If we begin with a sense of the world of the replicants as complex, internally coherent and common to them, but as far beyond our grasp as the world of a photograph (or film) is from the world of its viewers, then this sequence forces us to experience the impossible transition from our world to theirs – or more exactly, it forces us to recognize that, since we have made that transition, the idea that it was impossible might itself be a function of our prejudices rather than our knowledge. To accept the results of the analysis as genuinely revelatory is to accept that we might take up a position not on, as if from outside, but rather within the replicant world – and so that we must shoulder whatever new opportunities and burdens might result from the relation between our position and those of its other inhabitants.

This discloses the first range of significance derivable from the fact that the pivot of Deckard's (and so our) impossible transition between perspectives or worlds is a blown-up image of Zhora's sequinned dress. For suppose we follow Deckard in associating those sequins with the scale he recovered from Leon's bathroom. Then Scott is inviting us to associate Zhora's second skin with the skin of artificial animals, and so to think of replicants as beings who exactly resemble their natural counterparts, except with respect to their origins. So we might ask: what difference does such a difference in origins actually make? When, for example, we see Zhora or Leon or Pris suffering pain, are we prepared to acknowledge its reality as pain? Or must we rather think of it as 'pain' – as indistinguishable in any specifiable respect from the pains we human beings feel, but yet essentially distinct from them? As viewers of this film, how – if at all – should our responsibility to acknowledge Roy's pain differ from our responsibility to acknowledge Deckard's pain? Come to think of it, how exactly can we, and should we, respond to Deckard's pain? After all, even if there is no distinguishable respect in which he appears to differ from a real person, he isn't real, is he? Just what is it to acknowledge a projected, screened human being?

But of course, Zhora's dress is also very likely a part of her exotic act, at once seductive and transgressive; and the snake with which its sequins associate her is a key prop or assistant in her dance, in which (as the nightclub announcer will later tell us) they re-enact and exemplify humanity's original corruption and fall in the Garden of Eden. This might seem to reinforce the idea that Deckard's impossible transition from one coherent and self-sustaining world (in which the photograph has its place) to another (which that photograph makes present and even habitable in all its glory, despite its undeniable absence) is another Fall – from the moral purity of blade runners to an identification with the criminality they oppose, and one facilitated by an identification with a woman (one whom Deckard will soon seduce, dictating to her the requests he wishes to respond to, however much he might wish to claim that he was himself seduced). But then we need to recall that what we know as genuine humanity is postlapsarian, and that making sense of the idea of Paradisal life as genuinely human has proven notoriously difficult. Perhaps, then, we should rather regard Deckard's Fall as his acquisition of humanity, not as the moment at which he sloughs it off.

10) If we, as viewers, accept as coherent or intelligible the impossible shift of perspective implied by the final phase of the Esper analysis, and in this sense enter into the world of Leon's photograph as naturally and unresistingly as does Deckard, what – finally – does that suggest about our relation to the world in which Deckard himself undergoes that impossible experience? What are we to make of the fact that, by constructing an ultimately unrepresentable nesting of instances of subtly divergent kinds of representation (a moving picture of a computer-generated image of a painterly photograph of a reflection of a reflection of a living replica of a woman), this film seduces us into experiencing an impossible transgression of boundaries between representations, and between representations and what they represent? Here, it is worth emphasizing that the moment at which sense gives out in this wilderness of mirrors is the moment at which the image of Zhora's dress is so enlarged as to be barely recognizable; what fills Deckard's monitor screen, and so our own, at that crucial point is more accurately described as the ravishing glitter of a braid of reflective surfaces enhanced to the very limits of coherent resolution. And Scott cuts between this blur and a close-up of Deckard's bemused eyes, implying thereby that Deckard is mesmerized by the sight – as the client or victim of a professional hypnotist might be mesmerized by a brightly reflective coin or watch or ball spinning in bright light. Since – if or insofar as – we share this fascination,

Scott thereby declares his own internal relation to such a hypnotist, acknowledging that he too is in the business of exploiting our capacity and willingness to be hypnotized by blown-up, glittering images emerging from and within darkness: the interwoven skeins of projected light on a cinema screen. On the one hand, by stressing the material basis of the image over what it is an image of, he declares that the thing we see on the screen is not the thing itself; but on the other hand, by nevertheless leading us beyond that empty dress or sloughed skin to the living, breathing (replicant, but not therefore not) human being that inhabits it, and to an acceptance of her as there to be found in the photograph (beyond any practical obstacles or conceptual proscriptions), he declares that one can acknowledge that a film is a film without denying that it is (impossibly, but undismissably) capable of presenting us with reality, and with the full richness of human reality at that.

Notes

1 Both quotations are taken from Paul M. Sammon's unfailingly useful *Future Noir: The Making of* Blade Runner (1996, pp. 120 and 146, respectively).

2 The still photograph was in fact originally extracted from motion footage; and in order to create the effect of momentary motion, the filmmakers simply returned to a freeze-frame close-up of the relevant section of that footage and ran it forward briefly. Cf. *Future Noir*, p. 255.

3 As it happens, what we see on the Esper monitor was actually created by manoeuvring a motorized still camera attached to a camera dolly through a three-dimensional, fully furnished set of the replicants' two or two-and-a-half hotel rooms; the resultant still images were then rephotographed on motion picture film. Cf. *Future Noir*, pp. 258–9.

4 Cf. Cavell (1971, p. 23).

5 The right-hand door from the viewpoint of someone standing in front of it and facing it.

References

Cavell, S. (1971) *The World Viewed*, Cambridge MA: Harvard University Press.

Sammon, P. M. (1996) *Future Noir: The Making of Blade Runner*, Orion: London.

Chapter 7

Amy Coplan

IN THE MOOD FOR THOUGHT

MOOD AND MEANING IN RIDLEY SCOTT'S *BLADE RUNNER*

A film is – or should be – more like music than like fiction. It should be a progression of moods and feelings. The theme, what's behind the emotion, the meaning, all that comes later.

Stanley Kubrick

Introduction

The formal element of *Blade Runner* for which it is most famous and which has received the most attention from critics and scholars is the physical world – the dark urban future of a polluted, oversaturated megalopolis with neon lights, monolithic buildings, gigantic animated billboards, congested air space, streets teeming with people and activities, and layer upon layer of visual and aural complexity. Although this dimension of the film gets praised more than any other, its role in the film *as a whole* has rarely been fully appreciated.[1] The environment of *Blade Runner* is more than a setting or a background, though it is also those things. It forms a key part of the story and plays a critical role in how we make sense of and experience the characters and events. Moreover, the experience elicited by this world is itself part of what makes *Blade Runner* distinctive and part of why it continues to generate new interpretations and analyses. In addition, this experience exemplifies what film can do better than any other form of art.

In this paper, I examine some of the ways in which the formal elements of the film influence how we experience and interpret its meanings. More specifically, I consider how the film's use of stylistic conventions of *film noir*, moving light, and an extremely detailed environment and atmosphere express and elicit mood responses in viewers, which influence the way viewers proceed to engage with and interpret the film. I argue that the formal elements lead viewers to adopt an active stance in viewing the film by creating an ominous mood of paranoia and uncertainty.

Mood

Over the past few decades there has been a great deal of work within philosophy and philosophy of film on the nature and importance of affect and affective engagement with art. We now have a far better and more complex understanding of the roles certain affective states play in our experience of art in general and film in particular. However, the majority of this research concerns so-called standard emotions, such as fear, disgust, and surprise. Much of the focus is on cognitive processes said to be involved in emotion and on the ways in which these processes impact affective experience. Mood has received very little attention. Usually, it doesn't get mentioned at all. When it does, it is often treated as unimportant due to its non-cognitive or non-directed nature. I argue that this is a mistake. Moods constitute a significant dimension of affective experience, and perhaps an even more significant dimension than standard emotions. We experience moods more frequently than we do standard emotions, and according to some psychologists, mood may be more important for understanding the interaction of cognition and affect than standard emotions (Gray and Watson 2001; Watson 2000).

What is mood? Mood is an affective state involving physiological arousal and usually distinctive phenomenological feelings. Paradigm cases of mood include anxiety, depression, cheerfulness, dread, and irritability. Moods are related to emotions but possess a number of characteristics that make them distinct.[2] Moods lack the directedness (or intentionality) typically associated with emotion, which is usually thought to have a particular object. Moods can have nothing as their object or everything as their object. Thus if I am in an anxious mood and you ask me what I'm anxious about, I may say that there is *nothing* that I'm anxious about or I may say that I'm anxious about everything. If I'm experiencing an emotion rather than a mood, then according to most researchers my emotion is directed at a specific object. So if I feel fear and you ask me what I'm afraid of, assuming that I have reasonable self-knowledge, I should be able to identify a specific object (e.g. I may be afraid of not meeting a writing deadline, afraid of clowns, or afraid of spiders).

Another feature of mood that differentiates it from emotion is its duration. Prototypical emotions are brief, lasting for a few minutes at the most and usually for only a few seconds. Moods, on the other hand, can last for hours, days, and even longer.[3] In addition to lasting longer than standard emotions and lacking directedness, moods are more global or more globally oriented than emotions. Mood is a more diffuse phenomenon than emotion, which is thought to have a discrete or localized focus. In the case of mood, our feelings are generalized, influencing our overall experience and providing a kind of filter through which we experience the world and events in it. When we are depressed, for example, that depression generally affects the way we feel about everything so that the world seems to us to be a gloomy place. Our depression thus infects our experience in general rather than our feelings and attitudes toward a particular object, event, or person. Perhaps it is in part because of the diffuse nature of mood that some psychologists regard mood states as summarizing the overall state of the organism. While emotions typically focus our attention and reveal how we interpret a particular object or event, moods reflect how we are doing in general, that is, they provide a gauge of our global well-being.

Moods have a number of important effects. First, they lower the threshold for mood-consistent emotions and raise the threshold for mood-inconsistent emotions (Ekman 1994; Gray and Watson 2001). This means that when one is in a particular mood state, he is much more likely to experience emotions consistent with that mood state. If one is depressed, he is more likely to experience sadness and less likely to experience joy. If one is irritable, she is more likely to experience anger and less likely to experience amusement.

This feature of mood is worth highlighting as it demonstrates a critical way in which our low-level affect alters our experience of the world. Events that wouldn't normally elicit an emotion in us now do so easily. Many of us seem to have an intuitive awareness of this feature of mood;

when we know that someone is in an "irritable" mood, we "tip-toe" around her because we know that something that would normally be of minimal concern may arouse her anger, be it something as trivial as the dog jumping up on her, the batteries in the remote control going dead, or the mail being delivered later than usual. And yet in spite of our ability to recognize this tendency in others and possibly even in ourselves, we too are subject to the same type of behavior. We may realize that we are too easily angered due to being in a bad mood and yet this does not prevent our anger from flaring up on the basis of very little. Another way to characterize this feature of mood is to say that mood inclines us to make sense of the world in a way that permits or even encourages emotional responses.[4]

Mood affects more than just our affective and emotional experiences. It also alters the way we think. One way it does this is by altering our information-processing priorities. Moods increase our access to mood-congruent memories and associations and decrease our access to mood-incongruent memories and associations (Davidson 2004; Forgas 2007; Forgas and Vargas 2000). Individuals who are depressed are more easily able to recall sad memories and make sad associations and have a more difficult time recalling happy memories and making happy associations. Put simply, when we're depressed it's easier for us to remember and think about depressing things and it's harder for us to remember and think about happy things. This helps to explain why it can be so frustrating to be around depressed people and why it can be so difficult to deal with depression.

Mood also affects the style of our cognitive processing. Researchers have found that individuals in a cheerful mood typically have greater cognitive flexibility and creativity than depressed individuals. They are also more aware of and responsive to peripheral cues in their environment. In addition, individuals in a cheerful mood experience increased activation of relatively inaccessible mental concepts (Watson 2000; Parrott and Spackman 2000; Fiedler 2001; Bless and Fiedler 2006). One more way that mood influences cognitive processes is by altering the scope of attention. Positive moods broaden attention, and negative moods narrow attention. Finally, mood has effects on learning; researchers have found that mood-congruent learning is easier (Ellis and Moore 1999).

Elements of film noir

One of the major ways in which *Blade Runner*'s form expresses and evokes mood is through its use of numerous conventions of traditional *film noir*, which is something that few, if any, science fiction films had done before, though many have done so since. The precise meanings and applications of the terms *film noir* and *neo-noir* (the term used to describe more recent films made in a similar style) are the subject of ongoing debate, but both terms are often used to denote a distinctive visual style or a particular type of narrative or thematic content. *Film noir* is strongly associated with particular moods and feelings. Paul Schrader argues that it differs from western and gangster genres in not being defined "by conventions of setting and conflict, but rather by the more subtle qualities of tone and mood."[5] What kind of tone and mood? Typically, *noir* films convey feelings of paranoia, instability, insecurity, and alienation. They present us with a world that is full of decay, pollution, rain, and darkness, and in which many of the characters are haunted by some unseen threat. Wheeler Winston Dixon writes that "*Film noir* is the cinema of paranoia, of doubt and fear and uncertainty."[6] The visual style that expresses this encompasses a range of characteristics: high-contrast lighting, which has a chiaroscuro effect; fractured lighting that produces shafts or ribbons of light; scenes that take place and are shot at night; deep-focus shots that often rely on wide-angle lenses; location shooting; shots in which our view of the characters is often obscured by objects in the frame or by dark shadows; chaotic *mise en scène* that is often emphasized visually; liberal use of neon lights; lots of extreme low- or high-angle shots; and a characteristic set of symbols and motifs that includes nighttime streets, rain, smoke, people dwarfed by décor, hotel rooms, bars, diners, and images of urban decay.[7]

Blade Runner beautifully illustrates how effective these stylistic characteristics can be in producing a palpable sense of doom and the sort of ominous mood that are the hallmarks of *film noir*. But it is also a science fiction film that incorporates a variety of futuristic elements, which helps to explain why it is often described as "future *noir*."[8] And yet even though *Blade Runner* is a hybrid film when it comes to genre, it nevertheless provides a textbook example of the modern urban *noir* film. This is evident in the overall formal style of the film and especially in Ridley Scott's and cinematographer Jordan Cronenweth's lighting design and execution.

In an article on the production design and photography in *Blade Runner* that was published just as the film was being released, Cronenweth discusses his stylistic preferences and the different techniques he utilized when filming *Blade Runner*. Although he never refers explicitly to the film or to his style in terms of *film noir*, there can be little question that his formal choices would result in the mood and atmosphere that define *noir* films. Perhaps the most important example of this is Cronenweth's use of high-contrast lighting, which characterizes almost every scene in the film. He has a strong preference for shooting scenes with lots of backlight and contrast and in very low light, using a fast film stock in order to do so. When a shot is backlit, the light in the scene comes from the rear part of the set, which results in the figures in the foreground being cast in semi-darkness or silhouette.

The emphasis in backlit shots is often on the environment or atmosphere. While many cinematographers backlight a few scenes in a film, very few incorporate backlighting as often as Cronenweth did in *Blade Runner*. But unlike many cinematographers who were working at the time that the film was released (and many working today), Cronenweth did not view lighting actors' faces as his top priority.[9] On the contrary, as Patterson and Lightman explain, "Cronenweth is as interested in creating a mood or an effect as he is in lighting an actor's face."[10] Cronenweth himself says, "I can never get enough backlight. It's just that some directors want to see the face."[11]As a result of this preference, a remarkable number of scenes in *Blade Runner* are shot so that the actors are either silhouetted or cast in a semi-darkness with one side of the face hidden in shadow. Nevertheless, the lighting schemes are always designed so that there is enough visual information on-screen for us to make out the characters' faces. One way Cronenweth achieves this is by incorporating in the scenes a variety of light sources that allow for characters' faces to be lit from below with a soft front-light or under light (i.e. a fill light). For example, in one of the exterior scenes of the overcrowded city streets, there are people carrying umbrellas that have fluorescent tubes incorporated into their handles which provide a light source that can cast a glow on the people's faces.[12] In other scenes, one of which I discuss below, Cronenweth used water or reflective surfaces to light characters' faces from below. This style allows the film to be very dark while still presenting a great deal of visible information.

Figure 7.1 Still from *Blade Runner* (Final Cut) Dir. Ridley Scott (2007)

Another significant lighting technique Cronenweth uses throughout the film that helps to infuse the world with an ominous mood and a sense of paranoia is to combine very low light overall with carefully projected shafts of light that create ghostly visual patterns that give the suggestion that the characters are doomed or trapped. We get a striking example of this in the scene between Rachael and Deckard at his apartment. Upset by what Tyrell has told Deckard about her, Rachael wants to see Deckard. She tries to show him a photo of her mother, as proof that she has a history, and he responds by describing a private and personal memory of hers about playing doctor with her brother when she was six years old. Rachael says nothing. Deckard then starts to tell her about another memory – this one about an orange spider with green legs that lived in a bush outside her window. Rachael interrupts him to finish describing what happened. As she does, she steps forward and out of the dark background. We get a medium close-up of her, though the room is so dark that she is almost, though not quite, in silhouette. On her right is a window. The closed blinds filter the light that streams in and cast a shadow onto the low ceiling above Rachael. The shafts of light that are created frame Rachael so that she appears to be enclosed by bars from the side and from above. Revealing no concern or feeling, Deckard tells Rachael that her memories are implants, causing her entire world to unravel. She is then shown in close-up, with tears beginning to form. The pattern of the light is even more noticeable. It's as though she is in a cage.

In any given scene in *Blade Runner*, an enormous amount of information – visual, aural, narrative, and so on – is presented, and it's virtually impossible for us to take it all in. Moreover, our attention may be partially occupied thinking about the previous scenes or attempting to draw connections among the events and characters in the story. In addition, viewers vary greatly in their sensitivities to different elements of form. It could therefore be argued that the details of the lighting in a shot that is on-screen for only a few moments are not essential to our experience of the film. After all, many viewers won't even remember how a scene is lit or where and what kind of light is used. But these kinds of details are more powerful than it may seem.

Much of how we experience formal elements of film such as lighting is determined by our unconscious and automatic perception of the images and sound. We need not consciously attend to the lighting in order for it to generate an affective response. In many, if not most, cases – both when we are viewing a film and in the course of our daily lives – we are unaware of why we experience particular affective responses. They can derive from a broad range of stimuli, including the sounds we hear or don't hear, the shapes, colors, and movement we see, the amount of direct sunlight we experience, or the people with whom we come into contact. We are often completely unaware of the ways in which our environments influence our affective experience. But our ignorance of their causes does not make these affective responses any less real, and they will impact our subsequent thoughts and feelings regardless of whether we know their origin or even that they are occurring.

This feature of our psychology matters for our understanding of film in general and for our understanding of particular films, for film engages us in many ways that are outside of our conscious awareness but that may exert an influence on how we make sense of our overall experience. By lighting shots and scenes for strong affective impact, Cronenweth and Scott cause the environment and the light in the story to shape the way we go on to watch and interpret the meaning of the film. And the filmmakers use this lighting scheme of darkened spaces pierced by fractured light repeatedly throughout *Blade Runner*, as, for example, during Holden's interview of Leon at the Tyrell Corporation; in the scene at the police station when Bryant shows Deckard projected images as he briefs him on the escaped replicants; in almost every scene that takes place in Deckard's apartment; when Deckard searches Leon's hotel room; and in the scenes in the interior center court of the Bradbury Building, with its geometrically patterned staircases that are lit by searchlights coming in through the skylight. By repeating this lighting scheme in different scenes, Scott and Cronenweth sustain and reinforce the gloomy and uneasy feelings that we experience, which compel us to remain active as we search the screen for answers and actively contemplate the implications of what's happening in the story. Our mood fosters a sense of uncertainty, which leads us to be vigilant and alert.

Thus far, I have analyzed only a tiny fraction of the formal qualities of *Blade Runner* but I hope this is enough to make clear why the formal features and design of the film are instrumental to the story and our experience of it. We are dramatically affected by the visual and aural presentation of the plot, so much so that form and content cannot really be understood in isolation from one another. Indeed, the relationship between form and content in *Blade Runner* resembles the one created in Orson Welles's *Citizen Kane*. In both films, questions arise that never get answered, and the form through which the content is presented demands that we adopt an active stance in relation to the story. Both films are also paradigmatic cases of *film noir*, which is defined, in part, by its creation of worlds in which it is difficult to discern the truth but about which we are compelled to try to do so nonetheless. The cinematography in *Blade Runner* was influenced by *Citizen Kane*. In discussing the look of *Blade Runner*, Cronenweth said that Scott told him that the style of *Citizen Kane* was the one most closely approaching the one he was aiming for in *Blade Runner*.[13]

Light and its effects in the scene in Tyrell's office

One of the most distinctive features of *Blade Runner* – cinematically speaking – is its use of moving light sources, which appear in many scenes. As I explain below, the effect of the moving light on the viewer varies depending upon how it looks and functions within the scene, but in almost all cases it attracts viewers' attention and shapes the way they respond. In many cases, shafts of light, such as those I discuss above, move throughout a space. They usually take the form of a powerful beam that shines into an interior space. According to Cronenweth, he and Scott were able to justify the presence of these invasive lights due to the heavy air traffic that had been shown in the city. Both advertising ships and police vehicles would have powerful searchlights moving through the darkness at all times and making privacy impossible.[14]

Tyrell's office contains more open space than any of the locations we have seen up to this point in the film. The room is wide and open with high ceilings and an unobstructed view of the horizon and the world below. High-contrast lighting gives the scene a dramatic feel, which is intensified by the warm amber glow of the background light. The first interior shot of the office is of an owl, which flies across the room from one perch to another. Next, we get our introduction to Rachael, who asks Deckard if he likes the owl. The room is dark, and the light behind the owl and then behind Rachael is scattered, as it reflects off water from a source that is never shown directly. As Rachael walks into the center of the room to talk to Deckard, her costume, make-up, and hairstyle all bring to mind the *femmes fatales* of classic *film noir*. Just before she stops moving, she walks through a shadow bar created by the dramatic light. This provides a visual marker of her movement from a place that is hidden into one where she is more exposed.

As Rachael talks to Deckard, she is shot in medium close-up with the same glimmering light behind her. Next, we get a wide shot of Deckard and Rachael in profile in front of the window; in this shot, there is so little light upon them that they are almost completely in silhouette. When the camera then cuts to another medium close-up of Rachael, the light behind her is once again moving, though the effect is somewhat less noticeable than before. The moving light that accompanies the introduction of Rachael has at least two important effects. First, it creates a sense of mystery and otherworldly beauty, which is strengthened by the sound design, which calls to mind tinkling chimes. Second, the glimmering interferes with our attempt to focus intently on Rachael by

Figure 7.2 Still from *Blade Runner* (Final Cut) Dir. Ridley Scott (2007)

attracting our attention and directing it away from a fixed point on Rachael's face. As a result, we're unable to concentrate fully on Rachael and are left feeling that we cannot quite make out what kind of person she is, what it is she wants, or what she thinks of Deckard.

By incorporating reflecting light into this scene, Scott and Cronenweth are able to direct viewers' attention in ways that are largely unconscious. This is possible due to the way that we naturally respond to the appearance of movement. Film theorists David Bordwell and Kristen Thompson refer to this fact to help explain how *mise en scène* can function to draw our attention and gaze to particular parts of the screen:

> Most basically, our visual system is attuned to perceive change, both in time and space. Our eyes and brains are better suited for noticing differences than for concentrating on uniform, prolonged stimuli. Thus aspects of mise-en-scene will attract our attention by means of changes in light, shape, movement, and other aspects of the image.[15]

Given this natural tendency, we cannot help but notice the water effect when it appears in the shots of Rachael. It divides our attention and shifts at least some of our focus away from Rachael's face to the light and the room behind her.

When we're introduced to Tyrell, moments after meeting Rachael, the same reflecting light appears behind him, and yet differences in the way that Tyrell is presented lead to a somewhat different affective response, which gives rise to a different attitude. Whereas Rachael has an elusive or mysterious quality, Tyrell appears more sinister.[16] Before we see Tyrell, we hear him, and, like Rachael and Deckard, are a bit surprised that he seems to have been in the room the entire time, observing from the shadows. As Rachael and Deckard discuss Deckard's work, we hear Tyrell say, "Is this to be an empathy test?" Rachael and Deckard both turn to look, and we then get a long shot of Tyrell standing in the shadows at the very back of the room. The glimmering light reflecting off water now covers far more space than before, and its movement is more pronounced. Although this interior space has been quite dark all along, when we first see Tyrell, it appears to be even darker overall, and this makes the contrast between the shadows and the glimmering, reflected light even stronger. We can barely see Tyrell at the back of the room, except for his thick and extremely distinctive eyeglasses that cover almost half of his face. The large lenses reflect light and seem to glow when Tyrell moves forward, almost creating the impression that a pair of disembodied eyes is coming toward us. This entire sequence occurs very quickly, in a matter of seconds, and yet it is long enough for us to register perceptually, even if not consciously. Just as the giant eye in the opening sequence looked out upon the city from above, so Tyrell seems to be lurking in the darkness, seeing without being seen.

As he advances into the room, Tyrell enumerates the physiological processes that the Voight-Kampff test measures: "capillary dilation of the so-called 'blush-response,' fluctuation of the pupil, involuntary dilation of the iris." Dressed in a tuxedo, wearing his peculiar eyeglasses, and with a rigid posture, he emerges as a kind of god-like scientist who is mildly curious and perhaps amused by what's happening. And yet the way Tyrell's entrance is lit, combined with his physical presentation, arouses an uneasy feeling that makes us suspicious.

These suspicions increase after Deckard has administered the test and is alone with Tyrell. After finally identifying Rachael as a replicant, Deckard expresses surprise, but Tyrell is unfazed. Smugly, he asks how many questions Deckard had to ask before he was sure. Over a hundred were required. This appears to delight Tyrell. Deckard, on the other hand, seems unsettled and pushes Tyrell for an explanation. Showing no emotion, except perhaps that of self-satisfaction, Tyrell responds to Deckard:

> Commerce is our goal here at Tyrell. More human than human is our motto. Rachael is an experiment, nothing more.

Up to this point in the exchange, there has been almost no light in the room. One side of Tyrell's face is lit from the side by the reflecting light that is now dimmer than before. The rest of his face is in darkness, and the background behind him is almost black. This creates an eerie feeling that influences how we process what we're learning and raises questions about what is not being revealed.

After dismissing Rachael as nothing more than an experiment, Tyrell explains to Deckard that they began to recognize strange obsessions in the replicants and so began "gifting" them with memories to make them easier to control. As he delivers these lines, Tyrell steps forward toward the camera. We get a close-up of his face, and notice a change in the light. He now appears to be almost entirely backlit, with the reflecting light more perceptible as it produces the glimmer effect behind him. This time, however, the movement of the light has sped up and creates a strobe effect that intermittently makes more visible the dark foreground, where Tyrell's face is shown in close-up.

Due to the short duration of this exchange, viewers are unlikely to be consciously aware of the character and movement of the light. Nevertheless, we perceive these formal features of the scene and register them at a bodily level. This alters our engagement with the film, creating certain affective associations with the characters, and planting doubt and suspicion in our minds. The form fosters a sense of uncertainty and intensifies the mood of paranoia that was established at the outset of the film. In subsequent scenes, we will be searching for information to confirm our suspicions or answer our questions, and our emotional responses to the characters will be shaped, at least in part, by the affective responses that have already been evoked.

Moving light

In a film widely recognized for its distinctive form, it can be argued that the single most distinctive formal characteristic is the way in which Cronenweth and Scott incorporate multiple layers of light in every single scene. Above I described examples where this was done with shafts of light and moving lights. In several scenes, Cronenweth and Scott combined these two techniques by using moving searchlights that emit powerful beams capable of invading all and any spaces. Cronenweth explains that he and Scott were able to justify their use of these moving light sources because of the established presence in the city of air traffic. Giant ships used for advertising or crime control are shown to have on their undersides powerful lights that interrogate the darkness in the same way that searchlights monitor prisons.

The impact of these lights is significant and complex. In the scene that takes place in Deckard's apartment after he has killed ("retired") Zhora and Rachael has killed Leon, an extremely powerful beam moves through the represented space every 30 or 40 seconds, illuminating whatever lies in its path. This makes visible layers of detail in Deckard's apartment, including the intricately ornate geometric wall tiles modeled on the tiles in Frank Lloyd Wright's Ennis House, the fixtures in Deckard's kitchen, and dozens of framed and loose photographs cluttered on top of the piano. But the light also feels invasive and disruptive, which, as Cronenweth explains, is by design: "The shafts of light represent invasion of privacy by a supervising force, a form of control. You are never sure who it is."[17] Just as with the glimmering light in Tyrell's office, the movement attracts our attention. In this scene, however, it provides a frightening reminder that Deckard and Rachael are not safe and cannot hide, even though they are in Deckard's apartment with the blinds closed. This intensifies the feeling of paranoia that was created within the first few seconds of the film by way of the brief shot of a giant eye reflecting the Hades cityscape and surveying all within it.

The searchlights have another important effect that derives from the fact that they are positioned far away from the characters and the room they are in. Lightman and Patterson report that gaffer Dick Hart came up with the idea of using a Xenon spotlight commonly used for night advertising and sporting events.[18] We perceive this distance due to our familiarity with light sources in our everyday lives and this has an important consequence for our overall sense of the world that's created. It tells us, in a way that our body registers, that the world in the film extends beyond the boundary of the frame. This potentiality of cinema is articulated by André Bazin ([1967]2005), who conceptualizes the screen as a window on the world, more of which would be revealed if we were to move the frame in any direction. This is critical for how we think about and feel toward the film. It creates a sense of vastness that conveys a feeling of being overwhelmed and watched and influences the way we evaluate what happens to the characters. It activates our imagination as we conjure up images and ideas of what is taking place off-screen. And we're prompted to do this by the feeling instilled within us by our perceptual awareness of the location of the light source in relation to the characters. We therefore sense to a far greater degree that they are in danger as they attempt to live their lives under the watchful eye that transcends the frame.

Conclusion

My analysis of some of the formal features of *Blade Runner* has only barely scratched the surface of this extremely complex and richly detailed film.

There is much more to be said about the film and its ability to elicit affective responses, as well as about the more precise relationship between the feelings and moods created by the film and the thoughts these provoke in relation to the characters' predicaments and to the implications of their experiences. Nevertheless, I hope that my discussion makes it clear how inseparable are our experience of the film's form and our experience of its content. Moreover, I hope to have begun to show that the way films make us feel plays a fundamental role in what and how they make us think. Philosophers have a tendency to overintellectualize human consciousness and to minimize the importance of affective experience and the body. Understanding our experience of art, especially film, helps to show what's wrong with this tendency. Our thoughts are shaped by our feelings at least as much as our feelings are shaped by our thoughts. And in the case of *Blade Runner*, many of the formal features put us in the mood to think.[19]

Notes

1 Important exceptions include Bukatman (2012) and Sobchack (1997). Several theorists focus on the city in *Blade Runner*, but very few relate the character of the city to the other dimensions of the film, with some even arguing that the world and the story do not fit well together.

2 Not all researchers agree that moods and emotions are distinct phenomena. Craig DeLancey (2006) defends a version of what he refers to as the "mood-identity theory," which holds that certain moods are emotions. More specifically, he argues that some moods are the continual or frequent presence of an emotion. DeLancey's view stands in contrast to the general understanding of moods in philosophy and psychology, according to which moods possess a number of characteristics that clearly distinguish them from emotions and justify conceptualizing them as separate phenomena. DeLancey contends that the supposedly distinctive characteristics of moods can be explained away and that his mood-identity theory provides a more parsimonious way to understand moods than the global-change theories of mood that dominate the current philosophical literature.

3 Greg Smith (2003) considers duration to be the primary feature of mood that distinguishes it from emotion.

4 Smith (2003) talks about mood as preparing us to have an emotional response by focusing our attention on the objects and stimuli that will lead to mood-consistent emotions.

5 Schrader (1972, p. 8).

6 Dixon (2009, p. 1).

7 On the debates regarding *film noir* and its characteristics and conventions, see McDonnell (2007), Dixon (2009), Park (2011), and Schrader (1972).
8 As in the title of Sammon (2007).
9 Steven Katz argues that there is too much separation of subject and environment in contemporary film due to the tendency of most directors and cinematographers to view photography of actors as the most important part of storytelling, "with location the equivalent of stage scenery appropriate only for establishing shots" (1991, p. 239).
10 Lightman and Patterson (1982, p. 722).
11 Quoted in Lightman and Patterson (1982, p. 722).
12 Ibid.
13 Lightman and Patterson (1982, p. 720).
14 Ibid., p. 723.
15 (2001, p. 189). See, also, Block (2001, pp. 125–52).
16 It should be noted that this is just one possible interpretation of how the formal choices and their effects can be understood. For a variety of reasons, not all viewers respond in the same way. I do not mean to suggest here, or elsewhere in my paper, that viewer response is universal or even close to it. Nevertheless, there is good reason to believe that certain types of reactions are more likely (e.g. that our gaze will be drawn to movement).
17 Lightman and Patterson (1982, p. 723).
18 Hart himself discusses the development and use of the Xenon lights in the featurette "The Light That Burns: Remembering Jordan Cronenweth," which is included as part of the 2007 Collector's Edition.
19 I am indebted to David Davies for his insight and support and for giving this project "more life" when it was well past its expiration date. He truly is *Le Fixeur*.

References

Bazin, A. ([1967]2005) *What is Cinema?*, vol. 1, trans. H. Gray, Berkeley, CA: University of California Press.

Bless, H. and Fiedler, K. (2006) "Mood and the regulation of information processing and behavior," in J. P. Forgas (ed.), *Hearts and minds: Affective influences on social cognition and behavior*, New York: Psychology Press, 65–84.

Block, B. (2001) *The Visual Story: Seeing Structure of Film, TV, and New Media*, Burlington, MA: Focal Press.

Bordwell, D. and Thompson, K. (2001) *Film Art: An Introduction* (6th edn), New York: McGraw Hill.

Bukatman, S. (2012) *Blade Runner (BFI Film Classics)* (2nd edn), Houndmills: Palgrave Macmillan.

Davidson, R. J. (2004) "Affective style: Causes and consequences," in J. T. Cacioppo and G. G. Berntson (eds), *Essays in Social Neuroscience*, Cambridge, MA: MIT Press, 77–91.

DeLancey, C. (2006) "Basic Moods," *Philosophical Psychology*, 19(4): 527–38.

Dixon, W. W. (2009) *Film Noir and the Cinema of Paranoia*, Edinburgh: Edinburgh University Press.

Ekman, P. (1994) "Moods, Emotions, and Traits," in P. Ekman and R. Davidson (eds), *The Nature of Emotion: Fundamental Questions*, Oxford: Oxford University Press, 56–58.

Ellis, H. C. and Moore, B. A. (1999) "Mood and Memory," in T. Dalgleish and M. J. Power (eds), *Handbook of Cognition and Emotion*, Chichester: John Wiley & Sons, 193–210.

Fiedler, K. (2001) "Affective Influences on Social Information Processing," in J. P. Forgas (ed.), *Handbook of Affect and Social Cognition*, Mahwah, NJ: Erlbaum, 163–85.

Forgas, J. P. (2007) "Affect, Cognition, and Social Behavior – the Effects of Mood on Memory, Social Judgments, and Social Interaction," in M. Gluck, J. R. Anderson, and S. M. Kosslyn (eds), *Memory and Mind*, New York: Lawrence Erlbaum Associates, 261–79.

Forgas, J. P. and Vargas, P. T. (2000) "Effects of Mood on Social Judgment and Reasoning," in M. Lewis and M. Haviland-Jones (eds), *Handbook of Emotions*, New York: Guilford, 350–68.

Gray, E. K. and Watson, D. (2001) "Emotion, mood, and temperament: similarities, differences, and a synthesis," in R. L. Payne, *Emotions at work: Theory, Research, and Applications for Management*, West Sussex: John Wiley and Sons, 21–43.

Katz, S. D. (1991) *Film Directing Shot by Shot: Visualizing from Concept to Screen*, Chelsea, MI: Sheridan Books.

Lightman, H. A. and Patterson, R. (1982) "Blade Runner: Production Design and Photography," *American Cinematographer*, July, 684–91, 715–32.

McDonnell, B. (2007) "Film Noir Style," in G. Mayer and B. McDonnell, *Encyclopedia of Film Noir*, Westport, CT and London: Greenwood Press, 70–81.

Park, W. (2011) *What is Film Noir?*, Lanham, MD: Bucknell University Press.

Parrott, W. G. and Spackman, M. (2000) "Emotion and Memory," in M. Lewis and M. Haviland-Jones (eds), *Handbook of Emotions*, New York: Guilford, 476–90.

Sammon, P. (2007) *Future Noir: The Making of Blade Runner* (2nd edn), London: Gollancz.

Schrader, P. (1972) "Notes on Film Noir," *Film Comment*, 8(1): 8–13.

Smith, G. (2003) *Film Structure and the Emotion System*, Cambridge: Cambridge University Press.

Sobchack, V. (1997) "Postfuturism," in V. Sobchack, *Screening Space: The American Science Fiction Film* (2nd edn), New Brunswick, NJ: Rutgers University Press, 223–305.

Watson, D. (2000) *Mood and Temperament*, New York: The Guilford Press.

Chapter 8

David Davies

BLADE RUNNER AND THE COGNITIVE VALUES OF CINEMA

I

THE IDEA OF 'FILM AS PHILOSOPHY' – film as a medium in which genuine philosophical work can be done and philosophical understanding thereby advanced – has been promoted recently by a number of philosophers – Noel Carroll (2006), Stephen Mulhall (2002) and Thomas Wartenberg (2007), to name but three. A prominent line of argument in support of this idea points out that philosophical inquiry itself is often conducted through the use of brief fictional narratives – 'thought experiments' – an engagement with which is held to further philosophical understanding. Cinematic fictions, it seems, might present narratives that serve the same kinds of philosophical purposes. This mirrors a line of argument offered for parallel claims concerning the cognitive, and more specifically philosophical, value of literature (see, for example, Carroll 2002). Whether literary and cinematic artworks can indeed be ascribed this kind of cognitive value in virtue of contributing to our understanding of the extra-fictional world, and whether this might justify the claim that such works 'do philosophy', are hotly contested issues that I have discussed elsewhere (Davies 2007, 2010, 2012) but that will be of only marginal concern in this paper. But a further related question is whether, if cognitive values of this sort contribute to the artistic value of at least some narrative artworks, there are nonetheless significant differences between literature and film as media for presenting thought experiments, and thus between the kinds of cognitive values that can be pursued in these respective art forms. This question, to which I shall return in the final section of this paper, falls in a long tradition of inquiry into medium-based differences between the arts.

II

Blade Runner is a particularly interesting case study in this respect. As is well known, the film's central characters and fictional world originate in Philip K. Dick's 1968 novel *Do Androids Dream of Electric Sheep?* (henceforth '*DAD*'). This shares with the film an interest in exploring what is clearly a philosophical preoccupation, namely, to cite Mulhall, the question of 'what it is to be a human being'. Dick, indeed, described his novel as motivated by 'the problem of differentiating the authentic human being from the reflexive machine' (2007: 244). However, as we shall see, Dick's novel and Scott's film, while they share certain characters and a general fictional background, are in salient respects very different explorations of this shared philosophical concern. If the works are indeed akin to philosophical thought experiments, which have been taken to work by mobilizing the intuitions and tacit knowledge of the receiver, they are clearly intended to mobilize significantly different – even contrasting – intuitions, and, thereby, to support significantly different conclusions.

Although *Blade Runner*'s credits state that it is based on *DAD*, there are many striking differences between the two fictional narratives, and much detail in the novel is omitted in the film. This by itself shouldn't surprise us, since it is to be expected in any adaptation of a literary text for standard cinematic presentation.[1] As Paul Sammon, author of the principal study of *Blade Runner*, states, 'novels are so much richer than films – many different plots, themes and characters – and how can you get all of that into one and a half hours?'[2] Thus we shouldn't read too much into the omission, from the film, of such elements in *DAD* as the 'religion' of Mercerism and the use of 'empathy boxes', the ubiquitous *Buster Friendly* television programme, and the 'alternative' police force itself run by replicants. Other changes also seem, by themselves, relatively insignificant. The film's title and its use of the term 'replicant' for Dick's 'android', for example, seem motivated more by marketing considerations than by thematic concerns.[3]

But what immediately strikes a reader of *DAD* already familiar with the film is the different manner in which the replicants are portrayed and the character of their interactions with Deckard. This seems significant both at the level of narrative meaning and in its implications for the thematic meaning of the respective fictions. In *DAD*, it is clearly Dick's intention that the replicants[4] are conceived by the reader as *non*-human. They conspicuously lack a trait characteristic of organic life forms in virtue of their evolutionary heritage: the capacity to fight for their continued existence when this is threatened. In *DAD*, the replicants meekly accept their fate at the hands of Deckard, and he observes that this resignation is to be expected (2007: 130). Roy Batty's death in the novel, where Deckard shoots him in the back as he attempts to hide, stands in stark contrast to his death in the film.

The replicants in *DAD* are also presented as engaging in gratuitous cruelty with no concern whatsoever for the suffering of their victims. Pris's curiosity moves her to clinically remove the legs of a spider to determine how quickly it loses the ability to walk, and she is aided in this 'research' by Roy, who holds a naked flame close to the mutilated spider's body. This lack of empathy is described as one of a replicant's defining conditions – it 'ha[s] no regard for animals . . . [and] possess[es] no ability to feel empathic joy for another life form's success or grief at its defeat' (Dick 2007: 30), 'no ability to appreciate the existence of another' (ibid. 40). This characteristic is all the more salient for the reader given the central role accorded to empathy in the representation of *humans* in the book. In *Blade Runner*, this enters explicitly only in the Voight-Kampff test administered to discriminate between replicants and humans, although even here it is only touched upon in passing that this is what the test is for. Empathy is thematized in *DAD*, however, whenever the relationship between replicants and humans is at issue. Deckard ruminates upon the evolutionary basis of the human capacity for empathy, and its implications for our treatment of other animals with whose fate we naturally identify (ibid. 28–9), while elsewhere in the text replicants are described as lacking even the ability to care about the fate of their fellow replicants (e.g. ibid. 99). The novel is replete with references to and examples of the central role in human culture of Mercerism, a pseudo-religion whose rituals involve the sharing of one's pleasures and pains with others through the 'empathy box'. In *DAD*, as in *Blade Runner*, Deckard develops certain feelings for some of the female replicants – the opera singer Luba Luft and Rachael – but on reflection he deems these feelings to be a character flaw, an irrational consequence of the empathic nature that is part of being human. After he has sex with Rachael, she admits to seducing him to trade upon his natural tendency to empathize even with replicants. She has successfully pursued this strategy with other 'bounty hunters', inducing them to give up tracking and retiring the products of the Rosen (Tyrell) Corporation. This, we reasonably infer, is one of the tasks for which she has been designed. After Deckard leaves her to 'retire' Pris, Irmgard and Roy, she goes to his house and murders his newly acquired goat, his most cherished possession. Deckard, at the end of the novel, claims that his experience with Rachael has only hardened his resolve to do his job in 'retiring' replicants.

What is the thematic meaning of this narrative, and what conclusions are we intended to draw as to what it is to be human and the relationship between humans and replicants? Clearly, it seems, we are intended to conclude that the androids, while intelligent, fail to be human because they lack the essential human capacity for empathy. Interestingly, this emerges from Dick's account of the origins of the book. He narrates that the idea came to him when, researching his earlier book *The Man in the High Castle*, he read the diaries of certain Nazis working in concentration camps and was shocked when one complained that his sleep was disturbed by the cries of starving children. Such persons, Dick states, have 'a mind so emotionally defective that the word human could not be applied to them'. The androids in *DAD* represent this kind of personality in what are outwardly human beings: 'in my mind, android is a metaphor for people who are physiologically human but behaving in a non-human way' (ibid. 245). Thus, in the novel, there is no question of the replicants somehow acquiring the capacity for empathy. Rather, the inability to feel empathy is one of their defining features. Contrasting his use of androids in *DAD* and Scott's use of replicants in *Blade Runner*, Dick states that 'to me the [novel's] replicants are deplorable. They are cruel, they are cold, they are heartless. They have no empathy, which is how the Voight-Kampff test catches them out, and don't care about what happens to other creatures. They are essentially less-than-human entities' (ibid. 262). The central issue for Dick is not the possible 'humanity', in a non-biological sense, of replicants, but whether, as in the case of Deckard, a biological human can somehow lose his own humanity – his capacity for empathy

– in wrestling with such noxious elements. For Dick, 'the theme of the book is that Deckard is dehumanized in his job of tracking down the replicants and killing them . . . He winds up essentially like they are' (ibid. 262). We may follow Berys Gaut (this volume) in using the term 'evaluative' to qualify 'humanity' when the latter is to be understood in this non-biological sense: to possess 'evaluative humanity' is to be disposed to feel and behave 'humanely' and empathetically towards others.

In *Blade Runner*, however, the intended conclusion is clearly that evaluative humanity in no way depends upon being natural rather than artificial creations. While evaluative humanity requires a capacity for empathic response to the fortunes of others, this capacity is one that can *also* be possessed by 'replicants'. Scott urges this conclusion upon us in part by the manner in which the replicants are portrayed in the film in their interactions with Deckard, and in part through the identity of Deckard himself. Rachael, in contrast to the manipulative and unfeeling character in the novel, is portrayed as being capable of real emotions. And Roy's death, so briefly dismissed in *DAD*, is the emotional and narrative climax of *Blade Runner*. He is portrayed as capable of deeply poetic self-expression, and apparently of feeling empathy for Deckard, whose life he saves. His death is marked by the ascent of the dove he has been holding, usually taken in such contexts as a symbol of the departing spirit.

However, the most powerful element in Scott's film shaping our intuitions in favour of the desired conclusion is Deckard himself, at least in the Director's and Final Cuts. Consider the closing sequence, where Deckard examines the origami unicorn left by Gaff. This clearly seems to refer back to Deckard's earlier imaginings of a unicorn. Taken in the context of earlier scenes establishing the theme of implanted memories in Nexus 6 replicants, this seems to imply that Deckard is himself a replicant, for how else could Gaff have known about his imaginings? Indeed, Scott describes this implication as so obvious that 'if you don't get it you're a moron'! And, as others have noted, this is only the most obvious of many clues in the movie concerning Deckard's 'replicant' status.[5] But, empathizing creatures that we are, we naturally tend to identify with the protagonist in a film unless something firmly directs us otherwise. In this case we see the fictional world largely through Deckard's eyes, and through his experiences. By the time that Deckard's status is revealed at the very end of the film, we are already committed to his evaluative humanity – since we empathize with what we take to be his own empathic feelings – and thus to the evaluative humanity of at least some replicants.

Thus, while Dick's concern is with the possibility of biological humanity in the absence of evaluative humanity, Scott's concern is with the possibility of evaluative humanity in the absence of biological humanity. The book and the film nonetheless agree in certain respects. For example, they agree that it is the capacity for empathic engagement that is distinctive of being (evaluatively) human. It is unclear whether they disagree over whether such a capacity *could* be possessed by artificially intelligent creatures, since this question is not addressed in *DAD*. Dick is only committed to the absence of such a capacity in *his* androids, given that their purpose is to represent the evaluative inhumanity of some biological humans. But *Blade Runner*'s positive thesis – that being a product of artificial rather than natural selection is no obstacle to possessing evaluative humanity – bears crucially on our assessment of the characters in the narrative. If it is evaluative humanity – certain capacities for broadly moral action – rather than biological humanity – a certain kind of physical make-up – that has moral import, then it seems that, if at least some replicants possess evaluative humanity, to retire such a replicant is to kill another member of one's moral community, something which deeply compromises one's own humanity. Dick's narrative, on the other hand, purports to show that one can compromise one's humanity even by hunting and killing automata that merely outwardly *resemble* beings having evaluative humanity.

III

Given those features of the narratives sketched above, it is at least prima facie plausible[6] to think of both *DAD* and *Blade Runner* as artworks that have, and are intended to have, a certain cognitive value through functioning as thought experiments. Before raising 'external' questions about such purported cognitive values, however, it is worth asking whether the narratives, so construed, are internally coherent. For, if they are not, then they cannot lead to rational revisions of our beliefs, which, some have argued, is a cognitive virtue of at least some thought experiments. The most commonly cited locus of purported incoherence in *Blade Runner* is Deckard's implied status as a replicant who is also capable of empathy. This obviously presents a problem if we assume, in line with *DAD*, that it is a *defining condition* of replicants in the story that they not be capable of empathy. But incoherence also threatens if, as the film implies, the Voight-Kampff test can discriminate between replicants and non-replicants. For if we also assume that what the Voight-Kampff test measures is the presence or absence of a biological precondition for empathy, then, if Deckard is a replicant, he must himself lack this precondition and be incapable of empathy. But Deckard in the film is plainly capable of empathy. If he were not, then his response to the killing of Zhora and his treatment of Rachael – for example, his obvious regret for telling her so brutally that her 'memories' are only implants – would be unintelligible.

But there is in fact no incoherence here as long as we take the physiological responses measured by the Voight-Kampff test to be correlated with the *human* empathic response to the joys or sufferings of other creatures, and thus to be a precondition for one who is *biologically* human to feel empathy. This allows that beings lacking biological humanity – replicants – may nonetheless exhibit the emotional responses and behaviours constitutive of empathy – and may therefore possess evaluative humanity – without exhibiting the physiological correlates of empathy in human subjects. Thus there is no obvious narrative incoherence in the idea of Deckard as a replicant. And, as Berys Gaut (this volume) has pointed out in making a similar point, if there were such an incoherence, this would apply equally to Rachael and Roy, who clearly exhibit empathy in the movie. Roy does so both in response to the 'retirement' of Pris and – on perhaps the most plausible reading of his motivation – in saving Deckard's life (see below).

Some have thought that if Deckard is a replicant this renders *Blade Runner thematically*, rather than narratively, incoherent. For example, Frank Darabont, director of *The Shawshank Redemption*, insists that 'the story really only works if Deckard is human. The entire theme of the movie, which is very sophisticated, unravels [if Deckard is a replicant]. The theme of the movie being the story of a man rediscovering his humanity. He goes through all this moral confusion and comes out the end of it a real human being again.'[7] Curiously, on Darabont's reading of the film, its theme is the precise opposite of the one Dick ascribes to the novel, which explores a man *losing* his humanity through tracking replicants.

I suggested above that, by availing ourselves of the distinction between 'biological' and 'evaluative' humanity, we can remove any apparent narrative incoherence in Scott's use of the 'replicant' scenario. But *Blade Runner* also presents us with the following question: if the capacity for empathy is *not* to be explained in purely biological terms – indeed, in evolutionary terms, if Deckard's reflections on these matters in *DAD* represent the stance of the novel – how *is* it to be explained? How can the replicants be capable of empathy if this is not something explicitly programmed into them? This question is not addressed in the film nor in its subsequent discussion by Scott. But the narrative coherence of *Blade Runner* surely requires that *some* plausible answer can be extrapolated from the film. I shall suggest such an answer by elaborating upon another little-remarked, but, I think, significant, difference between the novel and the film – the use of implanted memories in the Nexus 6 replicants. Such implanted memories are of course crucial to the narrative development in *Blade Runner*. They explain Rachael's ignorance of her status as a replicant, and ground Deckard's discovery that he too is one. But what function are they intended to perform by those who implant them, and what are the consequences of such false memories for those in whom they are implanted?

In the novel there is a brief reference to such implants when Deckard, asking how Rachael could not know of her status as a replicant, reflects that 'sometimes they didn't; false memories had been tried various times, generally in the mistaken idea that through them, reactions to testing would be altered' (Dick 2007: 57). Rosen confirms that this is indeed the case with Rachael. False memories clearly have no significant thematic or consequential role here, merely being a device used by the Rosen Corporation to protect its products from detection. In *Blade Runner*, however, false memories not only play a much more significant narrative role, but are also ascribed a very different function by Tyrell/Rosen. Asked, as in the novel, whether Rachael knows she is a replicant, Tyrell replies:

> Rachael is an experiment, nothing more. We began to recognize in them a strange obsession. After all, they are emotionally inexperienced with only a few years to store up the experiences which you and I take for granted. If we gift them a past we create a cushion, a pillow for their emotions, and consequently we can control them better.

Figure 8.1 Still from *Blade Runner* (Final Cut) Dir. Ridley Scott (2007)

Deckard immediately responds: 'Memories. You're talking about memories.' Implanted memories, therefore, are, in *Blade Runner*, a means for controlling the replicants through, as Tyrell puts it, 'providing a pillow for their emotions'. It is also implied that this is the role that *genuine* memories furnished by 'the experiences which you and I take for granted' play for non-replicants. But how do memories 'provide a pillow for the emotions', and how does this control the behaviour of both replicants and, by implication, non-replicants?

I suggest that, in the world of *Blade Runner*, memories provide a ground for something like moral agency by allowing an individual to develop a historical self-conception, a sense of an individual life, and thus of acting in a way that is true to that conception. Memories can thereby act as a control on action – provide, in Tyrell's words, a 'pillow' for the emotions. As moral beings, we are, in a Kantian sense, self-regulating, but the laws we give ourselves are dictated not by reason alone but by our sense of who we are and how, given this, we should act. Put in terms of a narrative conception of self, the salient question is whether I can accept the supplementation of the narrative in which I have embedded my past actions with the action I contemplate doing. Implanted memories are intended to play, for the replicants, the same role that real memories play for us. They provide a built-in basis for something like moral agency on *their* part by gifting them a sense of having a history, an individual life, and thus a sense of acting in a way that is true or false to that historical life. Deckard and Rachael, then, have been given implanted memories for such reasons. There are good circumstantial reasons to think that this is not the case with Leon, Pris, Zhora and Roy, however.[8] The only photographs we see belonging to any of them are Leon's photographs of Zhora and his hotel room, which preserve *real* memories. But while we do not know the nature of the other photographs that he holds to be precious, the fact that Roy and Pris clearly take themselves to be replicants – witness the initial discussions at J. F. Sebastian's flat, for example, and Roy's discussion with Tyrell – strongly suggests that none of their generation of Nexus 6s have implanted memories. This is why Rachael is described by Tyrell as 'an experiment'.

A number of things support this analysis of the relationship, in *Blade Runner*, between memory and agency. When Roy meets Tyrell, he confesses that he has 'done questionable things'. Such a confession presupposes a standard against which he can measure his actions.[9] We can also illuminate the reference to *real* memories in Roy's final speech after he saves Deckard's life. He speaks of the things that he has seen, and of the memories that will disappear with him. The point he is making is not that these memories have an intrinsic value that cannot be transmitted to others and cannot survive his own demise. Rather, such memories have value for Roy, as for us, through not only giving a structural dynamic to the narrative of an experienced life – providing the subjective basis for a sense of personal identity and worth through change – but also providing a standard of accountability that grounds the possibility of autonomous agency. It is in terms of what we take to be our most substantial actions and experiences that we get our sense of who we are, and thus of what is required to be true to who we are. Such memories provide 'a pillow for the emotions' because our emotions and the actions they dispose us to do can be critically constrained by the sense that, in feeling and acting this way, we are not being true to ourselves. It is in terms of this sense of one's distinctiveness and worth as a historical being – as the being who did that or experienced this – that one can hold oneself accountable for one's own actions.[10]

This interpretation of the significance of memory in the film allows us to answer our original question as to how replicants are able to develop a sense of empathy. The ability to construct a historical self capable of grounding standards to which one holds oneself accountable is in fact a *precondition* for developing empathy in the sense that bears upon the possession of evaluative humanity. For only if one has such a sense of the worth of one's own life can one then see such a value in the life of another, and experience another's joys and sorrows as elements within

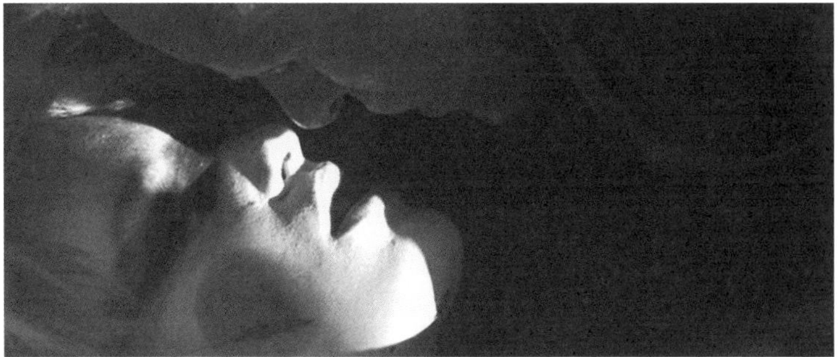

Figure 8.2 Still from *Blade Runner* (Final Cut) Dir. Ridley Scott (2007)

such a life. Empathy in the sense that bears upon the possession of evaluative humanity is a reflective achievement and not, as in *DAD*, part of our biological endowment that makes us passively respond empathically to what we encounter in experience. Reflective empathy is something that we develop, something not possessed by young children in spite of their natural tendency to empathically respond. In gifting Rachael and Deckard with a past in the form of implanted memories, then, Tyrell inadvertently gifts them with the preconditions for reflective empathy.

The key to Roy's capacity for moral action, therefore, is not empathy in the simple sense of 'fellow feeling', but empathy in the sense relevant to evaluative humanity – empathy grounded in a sense of himself as a being with a history of agency against which his actions are measured. It is his sense of the dignity and fragility of this life – grounded, it seems, in *real* rather than implanted memories – that explains his action in saving Deckard. He sees in Deckard another life, with its own history and sense of integrity, that faces extinction. The commentary included on the theatrical cut – written without input from Scott – says that at his end Batty is 'in love with life, anybody's life'. I would say rather that what his speech reveals is a recognition of a basic humanistic value, the value of a life having the dignity that comes with self-regulation, and of what is lost in its passing in death.

IV

In this final section, I want to broach a more theoretical question raised by the foregoing analysis of the thematic content of *Blade Runner* and

DAD. I have provisionally presented both fictional narratives as akin to thought experiments intended to elaborate upon ideas about what it is to possess evaluative humanity. As mentioned earlier, there is considerable controversy about whether narrative artworks can properly be seen as 'doing philosophy' in the way that the short fictional narratives offered by philosophers as thought experiments 'do philosophy'.[11] I want to bracket this question here and focus, rather, on the question of whether, and if so how, fictional narratives in literary and cinematic artworks – whether or not they count as ways of 'doing philosophy' – can possess cognitive virtue by serving as thought experiments.

The claim that literary and cinematic fictional narratives can possess such cognitive value is intended to counter what Noel Carroll (2002) terms the 'no-evidence' argument against the cognitive claims of the arts. Knowledge in general, the sceptic reminds us, requires not merely belief but belief that is *grounded*, either in reasons that we can furnish or in a reliable method of belief-formation. Art, on the other hand, it is claimed, moves us not rationally but affectively through its seductive manifolds. While engagement with an artwork may lead us to form new beliefs, the work itself furnishes us with no evidence for those beliefs. In response, it is claimed that fictional narratives can do serious cognitive work if they function as thought experiments. The latter are themselves short fictional narratives which are treated as instruments for cognitive advance in various branches of science, and are treated within the analytic philosophical tradition as a valuable resource for answering or better-understanding different kinds of philosophical questions. So, why shouldn't the more extended narratives characteristic of literary and cinematic works also, at least on occasion, serve as instruments of cognitive advance? (See, for example, Carroll 2002, Elgin 2007, Wartenberg 2007).

Such arguments for the cognitive value of artistic narratives might be challenged in at least three ways. First, one might question the cognitive value of thought experiments themselves. The literature in philosophy of science and in metaphilosophy presents serious challenges of this kind.[12] Second, it might be claimed that fictional narratives in literary and cinematic works differ in some cognitively relevant respect from the fictional narratives employed as thought experiments in scientific or philosophical contexts. Two possible disanalogies here are the purportedly non-cognitive goals of artistic narratives – the intention being to entertain or aesthetically engage the receiver rather than to intellectually stimulate or educate her – and their greater detail (Smith 2006). Third, even if we grant that literary fictions may serve a cognitive purpose, it might be argued that *visually* presented fictional narratives cannot. I have critically discussed these kinds of challenges elsewhere (Davies 2012) and it is unnecessary to rehearse these matters further here. I shall, however, briefly sketch some of the considerations raised by the third challenge, since it bears directly upon the question, raised earlier, whether literature and film can differ in salient respects as bearers of possible cognitive value.

Paisley Livingston has contested what he terms the 'bold thesis', according to which films can make 'creative contributions to philosophical knowledge . . . by means exclusive to the cinematic medium' (2006: 11). He argues that the insistence on exclusively cinematic means is necessary in any interesting version of the bold thesis. It is uncontroversial, for example, that one can make a film with philosophical content by simply filming a philosopher giving a lecture. The 'exclusive' features of the cinematic medium, he maintains, are visual features such as montage, editing and selective focus. But, he argues, cinema so construed can do philosophical work only through the mediation of linguistic paraphrase. This is necessary in order to locate the visual content of the film in a philosophical problematic. Taken by itself, film is philosophically mute. This objection, if valid, will apply equally to the more general thesis that film can present thought experiments, whether or not this counts as 'doing philosophy', because a thought experiment purports to stand in some kind of justificatory relationship to a claim. Thomas Wartenberg (2007), for example, defending the idea that cinema can 'screen' philosophy, endorses Tamar Gendler's claim (2002: 388) that to perform a thought experiment 'is to reason about an imaginary scenario with the aim of confirming or disconfirming some hypothesis or theory'. But this seems to require verbal mediation and thus, it would appear, resources that are not exclusive to the cinematic medium.

Some commentators on *Blade Runner* also seem to think that cinema has cognitive limitations, although they present this positively in terms of the distinctive affective powers of the medium. The novelist Jonathan Lethem, identifying Dick as a formative influence on his work, affirms that

> there's such a fundamental difference between film and fiction, and *Blade Runner* doesn't need to do as many different things with as many concepts and characters as the book because it's going to do something else instead – it's going to linger on us [sic] this unbelievably beautiful and strange and stimulating vision of the future and we wouldn't want to stop the movie from doing what it's doing panning over these streets and these advertisements in order to cram in something that's missing from the book – it's a perfect example of how those two forms have different requirements.[13]

The suggestion, I take it, is that cinema, as an essentially visual and affective medium, can engage the viewer perceptually and imaginatively rather than intellectually, providing us with images or experiences that remain with us and may inspire us to thought and reflection, but that do not themselves engage us cognitively in the process of watching the film.

This suggests, with Livingston, that a film like *Blade Runner* is not equipped to function as a thought experiment if it relies upon its exclusively cinematic resources, because the distinctive nature of the resources exclusive to the cinematic medium prevents a film from engaging unequivocally with a claim. Such engagement can only occur in our reflections *after* seeing a properly cinematic film, when we export from our experience a verbal representation of its contents and insert this into a verbally articulated problematic. Scott himself might be seen as giving some support to such a view, if we believe Dick's account of their exchange over the relationship between the book and the film. He reports that when he told Scott that the theme of *DAD* is that Deckard is dehumanized through his work tracking down the androids, 'Ridley said that he considered it an intellectual idea, and that he was not interested in making an esoteric film' (Dick 2007: 262).

I have argued elsewhere (Davies 2012) that Livingston fails to establish a principled difference between literature and film as media for presenting thought experiments with philosophical import. My contention is that the linguistic mediation necessary to perform a thought experiment is available in the resources internal to the cinematic medium, since the latter is essentially a *mixed* medium that usually incorporates both language and images. A film can articulate something by means exclusive to cinema when it articulates, through the *interplay* of the different resources internal to the medium, a content that is not articulated by the individual constitutive media – in particular, language – taken by themselves. This allows us to 'run' a thought experiment in our engagement with the film, rather than having to export from it something that only later can be situated in a verbally articulated problematic.

But, even if we resist the idea that cinema is constitutionally incapable of serving the kinds of cognitive ends served by a novel like *DAD*, certain distinctive features of *Blade Runner* raise genuine questions about whether it is fruitful to think about *Blade Runner* as primarily serving such ends. As noted earlier, Scott draws upon the viewer's tendency to identify with Deckard in order to establish in the viewer's mind the desired belief about the evaluative humanity of at least some replicants. But, in fact, this is just one instance of the viewer's more general tendency to empathize with characters in a film – even with cartoon characters and cartoon animals – insofar as they are visually presented as acting in the manner of human agents. The very human trait of reflective, and not merely instinctual, empathy – which, I have suggested, is the mark of evaluative humanity in *Blade Runner* – leads viewers to empathize not just with Deckard but also with the replicants. One might try to counter such a response by heavily stylizing the replicants' actions, but this cannot be done precisely because it is an essential feature of the story that replicants can only be discriminated from humans by very subtle tests – in particular, the Voight-Kampff test.

But then, it seems, the legitimacy of *Blade Runner* itself as a thought experiment is called into question. Given our empathic capacities, we naturally identify not just with Deckard but also with Rachael and Batty if they are naturalistically portrayed by identifiably human actors. Indeed, being the reflectively empathetic creatures that we are, how could we resist ascribing evaluative humanity to the characters played by Hauer, Young and Ford? But then how could a thought experiment that relied so heavily upon affective dispositions in the receiver provide rational support for the conclusion that artificially created intelligent forms really can possess evaluative humanity? How can our natural responses show that our natural responses are justified? Of course, it might be argued that the question whether replicants possess evaluative humanity is, like the question whether robots behaviourally identical and psychologically isomorphic to humans are conscious, a question that calls for 'a decision, not a discovery'. Hilary Putnam's reasoning (1964) with respect to the latter question might be enlisted in support of a parallel conclusion regarding the former question. Then we might claim, with Putnam, that the issue is really one of deciding who to admit to our moral community. But, if *Blade Runner* is to be read as part of a thought experiment for the evaluative humanity of replicants, the serious intellectual work will be done by the Putnamian reasoning. If the film plays a role, it must be a different one.

What might this 'different role' be? Here we may recall Scott's claim, cited earlier, that he did not wish *Blade Runner* to be an esoteric film with an intellectual content like Dick's novel. We can now observe that the 'intellectual' content sketched in section III above – the role that was ascribed to memories in providing a ground for the development of a sense of autonomous agency and, thereby, for developing a capacity for reflective empathy – was very much an extrapolation from what is explicit in the film. While there are resources in the film that allow us to explain how replicants might develop the capacity for empathy, this analysis is surely not something that would naturally present itself to the receiver in the process of viewing the film. In such a viewing, implanted memories serve merely to advance certain central elements in the narrative, and it is only in this capacity that they are salient for the viewer. This suggests that while, as I have argued elsewhere, there is no reason why the cinematic medium cannot be used to 'screen' a thought experiment, *Blade Runner* is not usefully viewed in this light, even though its literary progenitor serves such a function in its own chosen medium.

Rather, as Lethem suggested in the passage cited earlier, *Blade Runner* uses the unfolding of the narrative in the brilliantly crafted dystopic visual landscape to do something else. It affectively moves the viewer through a vision that remains with her – that 'lingers' – long after she leaves the cinema. It is part of the power of cinema that it can give us such experiences, and give us an experiential sense of things not available to us in reality. And this is a different way in which film can have cognitive value – not by 'screening' a thought experiment but by giving us a clearer grasp of the experiential dimensions of a philosophical issue. Murray Smith (2006), arguing against the idea that films can 'do philosophy', has suggested that philosophical and artistic fictions are intended to elicit different kinds of imaginings – 'hypothetical' and 'dramatic', respectively.[14] To hypothetically imagine something is to entertain a counter-factual in an abstract way, whereas to dramatically imagine something is, as he puts it, to 'try' on the hypothesis, to imagine inhabiting it, or to explore its implications rather than philosophically engage with it. The much greater detail in artistic fictional narratives, he maintains, is intended to promote dramatic imagining, in order to serve what are primarily non-philosophical purposes. For the purposes of philosophy, it is 'hypothetical imagining' that is required.

A work like *DAD* is, I think, plausibly viewed as intended to produce an extended hypothetical imagining. But dramatic imagining may also serve a properly cognitive, and even philosophical, function. In the case of *Blade Runner*, it might be said, the haunting detail conveyed for the most part through the visual manifold provides us with a much richer sense of what is at stake if the question whether replicants like Pris and Roy possess evaluative humanity indeed calls for 'a decision, not a discovery'. In Putnam's thought experiments on robot consciousness, it is obscure both what this 'decision' involves and what import it has. Scott's film provides much greater illumination as to what is involved in a related question – whether artificial life forms can possess evaluative humanity – and, correspondingly, what is at stake in the philosophical debates about the relative status of persons and of artificial forms of life. To treat an entity as possessing evaluative humanity is to admit it to one's moral community, to hold it responsible for its conduct, to feel both with it and for it. Here, dramatic imagining deepens our understanding of the philosophical issues, and it is in virtue of this deeper understanding that our intuitive responses to these issues are placed on a firmer rational foundation. Artistic cognitivism with respect to literature and cinema, then, is compatible with the acknowledgement that they may differ in their potential to perform various kinds of cognitive functions. And *Blade Runner* is among the greatest examples of a certain kind of potential in cinema.[15]

Notes

1 This is not to say that one cannot cinematically present a literary fiction in its narrative entirety. Indeed, this is something that can be achieved in a television series, as was done with Evelyn Waugh's *Brideshead Revisited*. The point holds, however, for any cinematic presentation intended to be viewed in a single sitting, usually in a cinema. I am grateful to Berys Gaut for pointing out the need to clarify this point.

2 This quote is taken from 'Sacrificial Sheep: The Novel vs the Film' on DVD4 of the Special Edition of the Final Cut of *Blade Runner* (Warner Bros and the Blade Runner Partnership 2007).

3 This seems clear from the history of the making of the film as documented in *Dangerous Days* on DVD2 of the *Final Cut: Special Edition* package.

4 For convenience, I shall use this term when talking about both the novel and the film, although, where appropriate, I shall also use the term 'android' in talking about the novel.

5 For other 'clues' and the quote from Scott, see 'Deck-a-Rep?: The True Nature of Rick Deckard', on DVD4 of the *Final Cut: Special Edition* package.

6 Prima facie plausible but, I shall argue in section IV, misguided in the case of *Blade Runner*.

7 In defence of this view, Darabont offers a somewhat implausible explanation of the scene with the unicorn: 'That's not his recollection. How on earth could that be his memory? It's not. He's thinking about Rachael, he's thinking about her implanted memories, he's thinking about her implanted fantasies. In terms of myth that is totally a *female* myth symbol. And at the end when Gaff leaves the little unicorn, that's not about, "oh Deckard, I'm wise to you, you're a replicant and I know what's in your head". It's Gaff's little grace note, you know, to Deckard, saying, "you know what, I think they're as human as anybody else, and if you're falling in love with her, man, go for it, run, get her out of here"'. For these claims by Darabont, see 'Deck-a-Rep?'.

8 I am grateful to Berys Gaut for raising this issue.

9 Tyrell's response completely misses the moral dimension to Batty's actions. He merely complements him on his various accomplishments that draw upon the aptitudes his makers have given him.

10 The idea that what one takes to be one's greatest experiences and achievements are the measure of the value of one's own life is wonderfully captured by Ezra Pound in his poem 'Erat Hora': 'Thank you, whatever comes'. And then she turned / And, as the ray of sun on hanging flowers / Fades when the wind hath lifted them aside, / Went swiftly from me. Nay, whatever comes, / One hour was sunlit and the most high gods / May not make boast of any better thing / Than to have watched that hour as it passed' (Pound 1968: 54).

The further claim that I am making is that it is this sense of the value in one's own life that can provide the standard to which one holds oneself accountable, and thus the basis for autonomous moral agency.

11 See, for example, Russell 2000; Livingston 2006; Smith 2006; Carroll 2006; Wartenberg 2007.

12 See, for example, Duhem 1954; Hempel 1965; Norton 1996. For critical discussion of these arguments, see my 2007 and 2010.

13 'Sacrificial Sheep', on DVD4 of the *Blade Runner: Final Cut: Special Edition* package.

14 Smith credits this distinction to Richard Moran. See Moran 1994.

15 I would like to thank Amy Coplan, Berys Gaut, Robert Hopkins, Shawn Loht and George Wilson for helpful comments on earlier drafts of this paper, the writing of which was supported by a grant from the Social Sciences and Humanities Research Council of Canada.

References

Carroll, N. (2002) 'The Wheel of Virtue: Art, Literature, and Moral Knowledge', *Journal of Aesthetics and Art Criticism*, 60.1, 3–26.

—— (2006) Introduction to the section on 'Art and Cognition', in Noel Carroll and Jinhee Choi, eds, *Philosophy of Film and Motion Pictures: An Anthology*, Oxford: Blackwell, 381–8.

Davies, D. (2007) 'Thought Experiments and Fictional Narratives', *Croatian Journal of Philosophy*, vii.19, 29–46.

—— (2010) 'Learning Through Fictional Narratives in Art and Science', in Roman Frigg and Matthew Hunter, eds, *Beyond Mimesis and Convention: Representation in Art and Science* (Boston Studies in the Philosophy of Science 262), Dordrecht: Springer, 51–70.

—— (2012) 'Can philosophical thought experiments be "screened"?', in Melanie Frappier, Letitia Meynell and James Robert Brown, eds, *Thought Experiments in Philosophy, Science, and the Arts*, London: Routledge, 223–38.

Dick, Philip K. (2007) *Do Androids Dream of Electric Sheep?* 25th Anniversary Edition, with an additional essay by Paul M. Sammon, New York: Ballantine Books. (The original edition of Dick's novel was published in 1968.)

Duhem, P. (1954) *The Aim and Structure of Physical Theory*, trans. P. Weiner, Princeton NJ: Princeton University Press.

Elgin, C. Z. (2007) 'The Laboratory of the Mind', in Wolfgang Huerner, John Gibson and Luca Pocci, eds, *A Sense of the World: Essays on Fiction, Narrative, and Knowledge*, London: Routledge, 43–54.

Gaut, B. (this volume) 'Elegy in LA: *Blade Runner*, Empathy and Death'.

Gendler, T. (2002) 'Thought Experiments', in the *Encyclopedia of Cognitive Science*, London: Routledge, 388–94.

Hempel, C. (1965) *Aspects of Scientific Explanation*, New York: Free Press.

Livingston, P. (2006) 'Theses on Cinema as Philosophy', *Journal of Aesthetics and Art Criticism*, 64, 11–18.

Moran, R. (1994) 'The Expression of Feeling in Imagination', *The Philosophical Review*, 103, 74–106.

Mulhall, S. (2002) *On Film*, London: Routledge.

Norton, J. (1996) 'Are Thought Experiments Just What You Always Thought?', *Canadian Journal of Philosophy*, 26.3, 333–66.

Pound, E. (1968) *The Collected Shorter Poems of Ezra Pound*, 2nd edn, London: Faber and Faber.

Putnam, H. (1964) 'Robots: Machines or Artificially Created Life?', *Journal of Philosophy*, LXI, 668–91.

Russell, B. (2000) 'The Philosophical Limits of Film', *Film and Philosophy*, Special edition on Woody Allen, 163–7.

Smith, M. (2006) 'Film Art, Argument, and Ambiguity', *Journal of Aesthetics and Art Criticism*, 64, 33–42.

Wartenberg, T. (2007) *Thinking on Screen: Film as Philosophy*, London and New York: Routledge.

Index

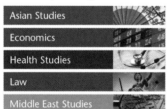